REA
ALLEN COUNTY PUBLIC LIBRARY
ACPL ITEM
3 1833 05168 5714
DISCARDED
S0-BWV-095

Snowed
A Lesson In Love

A Novel
By
Nishawnda Nicole Ellis

Kindle Eyes Books
Massachusetts

FEB 07 2007

Kindle eyes Books
P. O. Box 692092
Quincy MA 02269

This book is a work of fiction. Names, Characters, Places and incidents either are products of the Author's imagination or are used fictitiously. Any Resemblance to actual events or locales or persons, Living or dead, is entirely coincidental.

Copyright© 2001 by Nishawnda Ellis
All rights reserved, including the right of Reproduction in whole or in part in any form

Cover Designed by Jennifer Woodward
Edited by Judy Schuler

Printed in the U.S.A by Morris Publishing
3212 E Hwy 30
Kearney, NE 68847
800-650-7888
Fax: 308-237-0263

ISBN
0-615-12111-X

ACKNOWLEDGMENTS

On a down day at a nowhere job, little did I know that a little letter to myself would ignite this fire to create an entire book!

I would like to thank my mom, Phyllis, and my dad, Charles, who made me literally, but also created the person I am today.

Mom, your touch of class is somewhere in this book. And don't worry; I made all this stuff up, it didn't really happen!

Daddy your "I don't worry about Shit" way of life is definitely in there. Thanks for everything you do.

To my grandmother whose voice I hear in some of my characters, "Not a bit more than nothing!" I don't know where my life would have been if you hadn't been in it.

To my sister, Tiffanie, for letting me know that you can do 101 things at the same time, to get the job done and be and do anything you want to do. And, yes, I had to use your Tanya alias, sorry!

To my brother, Charles Jr., for having the biggest heart in the world, no matter how mean I can be to you. And no, I won't charge you for a copy.

To my little sister, Charnai, who has the potential to be anything she wants to be, even a writer like her big Sis! Just kidding, be you, because you are wonderful!

To the rest of my family, Reid and Ellis, because of you I know what a family really is.

To the ladies, Kizzy, you got it going on girl, no matter what you think. Krishona, be kind to your friends, not just the fellas, I love you anyway. Thanks for reading my book over and over again and letting me pick your brain over and over again. Don't worry; I will do the same for the next one! Ayana, your words of encouragement always move me in the right direction. Andrea, you are such an angel (AH HA)! Kenyetta are you with us or what? Stop zoning! I love you all, you are my DAWGS!

To Jamila, for being one of my sane, but still crazy friends. To Christina, Yaneke, Zakiya and Adam, my Hampton road dogs, who didn't say to me "Your major is nursing, not journalism, leave that book alone!"

And lastly but not least, thank you readers, who have supported this project and enjoyed this book as much as I have. I love you all, and I hope to have you laughing, crying and kicking yourself in the "you know what", in the next book.

Snowed
A Lesson In Love

CHAPTER ONE

"Why haven't you called me, Sasha? Are you mad at me" Jason said with contempt in his voice.

"No I'm not mad, I just…I just," I began, caught off guard by this call. *I thought you were over, damn it; if you don't call someone, you are not interested.*

"You just what? Forgot about me? I mean are you mad at me? What's the problem?" Jason rambled on and on about why I hadn't returned his call.

I mean we went out a couple of times and it was all right, but he was no keeper, no soul mate, not even sexing material. I just wanted someone to talk with, to take me out, and maybe fake for a while at the thought of this being the one.

For the longest, I was so grossed out by this love stuff. I wasn't into men. I was into TV and what movies were on, which ones were x-rated. I mean guys just didn't impress me. Even when I was dreaming about growing up, it was about being successful. A husband sometimes entered the fantasy, but that was only for one thing. I was not love oriented until I started watching soaps and those 80's brat pack movies, like *St. Elmos Fire*. Then, all of a sudden I was into boys.

I met my first so-called love. My high school sweet heart, the one to give up my virginity to. I thought he was cute, but he was no regular flavor of mine. He was caring, humble, and glad to even have the chance to talk to me. I was happy, because he was happy with me. He didn't know my dark side.

With him I thought I was queen, and could do anything; say anything, just act up and it would be okay. After I got a taste of that chocolate bar, I felt so free. I felt older, more mature and independent.

My dreams changed and I began to fantasize about romantic, and "I'm in love" things. I thought my love life would be like the movie *Boomerang* and *Menace to Society.* The guy was down for his woman, even though he messed up and she broke away. He would admit his faults, see where he went wrong, and realize she was the best thing that ever happened to him. That was my idea of true love. So I pretended I had that with Chris. I fantasized him as being the one who would never fall out of love with me.

While I was in fantasyland, Chris cheated on me so that was my out of the relationship. I had kind of wished he'd do something, so I could get rid of him. Somewhere down the road I realized that I didn't love him. He wasn't Mr. Right. He was Mr. Right Now. He loved me, but it wasn't storybook love. He was young and I was young. I have more control over love than that now. I think.

So as Jason rambled on, I finished meditating and said in a silly voice. "I'm not mad at you. I'm sorry I didn't return your call."

In a desperate attempt to win my favor Jason said, "Okay, is the snow really deep outside, because I was going to come over?"

I quickly stated, "Yeah it is very deep out, you shouldn't come over."

"I could walk it's not that far from here."

Walk, its knee deep in snow, is he crazy!

Jason continued, "I could probable ride my bike."

"NO!" I said with contempt. "Look, Jason I …"

"It's okay Sasha, I'll call you back," Jason interrupted. "You're not cheating on me are you?"

"WHAT!" I was so repulsed.

"I'm just playing, I'll hit you back." Jason hung up.

About time, he finally hung up. What is going on around here? I stopped calling Jason a month ago. If he calls me back I don't know what to do. He was just another bugaboo who couldn't help me in my search for my real love.

After hooking up the phone to the Internet so it wouldn't ring, I turned on the slow jams and walked into the bathroom. The shower was running and the steam fogged up the mirrors. I could see Damon's figure through the champagne-colored shower curtain. I thought *should I*?

Before I knew it Damon had opened the shower curtain and swept me up into the shower with my lavender lace and satin nightgown on. I wrapped my arms around him and lifted my weight to end up in his arms with my legs around him. I kissed him softly, before he could open his mouth. He kissed me back. He ripped my nightgown off and threw it over the curtain railing. Damon began kissing me all over. With one hand he held me up; with the other he closed the shower curtain. We dreamt and melted in each other's arms, as we made love for the rest of the night.

It was snowing outside, schools were cancelled and stores were closed. The hospital was open though, and I had to be there in three hours. Damon made me a vegetable and cheese omelet with toast. He knows exactly what a women needs; pampering, good conversation, and great sex. Damon is a keeper, if he could stop being such a ladies man. The arrangement we have is cool. Mr. Wonderful or not, he isn't the love-of-my-life type. He satisfies a hungry woman's belly, but not a dying woman's last request. He has his own thing going on, no matter how much he denies it. I know he sees other women, but I see other men. However, I'm not that dishonest about it. I told Damon, that I didn't want him to be my man, just a good friend. He didn't have to lie to me. However, he swore up and down that I was his wifey. Well, that can get tiring quickly, so I consider myself, occupying time and space in an empty heart. But of course, he sees it differently. I like Damon. I'm very fond of him. What we have is good for me. I work almost fifty hours a week trying to advance my career. I really don't have time for all the loving and nurturing a relationship needs. Damon doesn't either, he just wants someone to show off to and to make you think that you're his one and only. He isn't shallow but sometimes I can look into his eyes and swear all he sees in me is a pretty face. He doesn't really see me. His feelings didn't run that deep. He sees me as a commodity. He just has to have a badass girl. I play along with it for now, but like I said that can get tiring.

The next morning was messy. The snowy road had turned into dirty slush and huge piles of plowed snow. After working overnight, the first sight of daylight is kind of confusing. You think you're supposed to just be waking up and then realize you've been up for sixteen hours. I just wanted to reach the train station because I had forgotten my scarf and could feel the chill going down my neck. The cold wind smacked me in the face, reawakening me. Its days like this I miss Florida. It was warm in January. A scarf and boots were not needed.

Boston is always cold in the winter. I got spoiled while I was away at Florida A & M for my undergraduate education. The weather in Florida is unpredictable though. In the beginning of the week the weather is sixty degrees. By the end of the week, you are putting on gloves and hats and lined leather jackets. That is one of the reasons I returned home to Boston.

I am closer to my family now. These days they are all that matter to me. I've grown to appreciate them more. I wonder if Raymond made it home last night. I try not to mix business with family, but it never works. I agreed to let my brother, Raymond, rent my upstairs apartment, but on the condition he not stay there too long. I love my family, but I love them even more when they are away. Raymond isn't much bother though. As kids we bickered like any other sister and brother, and he knew how to irritate me. But he promised not to do that anymore. It's been working out so far. He hasn't brought any drama, like in the past.

Raymond was chilling. He went back to school and was coaching a middle school basketball team at the recreation center in Roxbury. He tried to get as close to his hoop dreams as possible. Basketball seemed like his only way out. Dreams of a million-dollar house, a million-dollar car and million-dollar girl seemed to be the only motivation for young men not interested in the academic path. Raymond loves the game because the game let him escape whatever he was running from. The thought of all that fame and glory soothed any other bad feeling that crossed his mind. He's been all right. Raymond and I understand each other. Even though we still may argue, he knows me better than I do. I know the hoop wasn't Raymond's heart, it was his safe point. Now he doesn't completely have that dream any more, but he can see it through someone else's life, and feel safe.

By the time I reached home, there was a policeman, an ambulance and my new VW Passat parked in front. I thought to myself, I know I wasn't robbed… my heart dropped, Raymond. I rushed up the stairs to my apartment following a trail of blood to the top. My heart was pounding. All kinds of thoughts ran through my head. I shouted, "Officer, I live here. What happened, where is my brother?"

The officer replied in a sneer voice, "*So he is your brother*."

My faced became crooked. "Officer…"

He took his finger and pointed toward the back porch. I walked slowly as though I was afraid to move. I didn't notice that my place was trashed. I didn't notice that the draft came from a broken window. As I reached the back porch, three officers stood around my brother. There he sat head bent to his knees, hands behind his neck and handcuffs around his wrists. The police had my brother shackled on my back porch wearing just a t-shirt and jeans in the middle of winter!

Before I blew up at someone, Raymond looked up at me and said, "I tried to stop him."

CHAPTER TWO

Okay by now I was getting upset. I turned toward the three officers who were on the porch. "Why do you have my brother in handcuffs? Get him out of those things immediately!"

"Well, Ma'am," one of the officers said, "We were under the impression that he was the other perp."

"Was that before or after he informed you he lived here?" I questioned.

"Look we have a job to do…"

"And just what is that job? To harass the innocent and let the guilty walk? You thought, no way could a young black man live in a place like this. He must be a thief, selling dope, or one of those entertainers."

"Look here lady, we were just doing what we thought was right."

"That is the problem, officer, you were not thinking." I walked toward the door, "Look, here is his mail, Raymond Freeman, 222 Willows Street…"

"Ma'am, we tried to identify him, but he had no identification."

"He didn't need any ID. His picture is right here on the wall."

"Ma'am…"

"Who's in charge here? You have completely acted out of bias and you have my only brother out here in below-zero weather with no coat, for god knows how long!!!" I raised my finger to point. "You didn't think, you reacted and your reaction was he had to be part of the crime because of who you see!!!"

"Ma'am, if you don't calm down, I will have to…"

"You will have to what? Arrest me, in my own home for what, speaking my mind? Who's in charge? You didn't even offer him a blanket. If I have the last word, you will be doing crossing duty for the blind! I demand to speak to someone."

"Ma'am, I…"

Just then a voice filled with bass, interrupted my rage. "I'll take it from here, Bob." A tall man entered the porch, flashed his badge my way, and began to speak as if he were in charge. "Ma'am, my name is Detective Perry and I'm in charge here."

I noticed his good looks, but didn't let it interfere with my anger. "So you're responsible for my brother being left out in the cold? I would expect different from…"

"From what? One of your own? Look lady, this is not a black and white issue, Officer Smith was just doing…"

"Yes, I know his job. But his job is to protect and serve, not to leave people out in the cold."

"Look lady I just entered the scene and …"

"My name is Ms. Freeman, Sasha Freeman."

"Well, Ms. Freeman, your brother's not going to be charged with anything."

"Charges!" My eye browses rose, "For what?"

"Well, he did assault the intruder. But I am sure no charges will be brought for that."

"Assault? He stops the intruder from stealing everything, and from the looks of my apartment he would have gotten away with it."

Raymond walked into the apartment. I gave him a blanket and asked if he were okay. He didn't complain, because he would never let someone know they got to him.

"I'm sorry for the mix up, Mr. Freeman, but the officer just wanted to make sure he covered all his bases," Detective Perry explained to Raymond.

Raymond nodded, "Whatever! I tried to stop him, Sash, but he had already gotten through the window and into the house."

"What happened, Ray?"

"I came home around five this morning and heard mad noise coming from your apartment. I knew you weren't home, so I used my key to check it out. He had already torn the place apart, but didn't take anything. I snatched him up, we fought and he pulled a knife. I managed to get it away, but I stabbed him."

"Don't worry about that Ray. Detective Perry has assured me that there won't be any charges."

"I did not assure, I said it's not likely," Detective Perry interjected.

"Well, it is your job to make sure that it doesn't. This is a clear-cut case of self-defense. The perp had no business in my place."

"Oh, so now we've moved from civil rights leader, to judge, juror and prosecutor."

"I am one phone call away from a lawyer."

"That kind of talk is hostile. Look, I told you, I'll do my best. In the meantime, I need you both to come down to the station to make a statement and press charges."

"What? Can't that wait? My place is a wreck, I just got home from work, and I am not in the mood."

"Oh well, that does it; she's not in the mood to make a statement. Let's stop the investigation. Everyone go home," Detective Perry said.

I folded my arms. "Do I know you?"

"Excuse me?" Detective Perry said, placing his hands on his hips.

"I mean, you talk to me as if we were past acquaintances or you knew me or something."

"Ms. Freeman, I will do what I can, but I need you to make a statement."

"You need me, Detective Perry?"

He gave a smile covered with dimples and surrounded by a look of defeat. He couldn't win with me. I don't know why he even tried. I noticed how handsome this man was, once I got past his arrogance. The way he wore his trench leather jacket and flashed his badge made him very sexy. I love a man in charge, not one who thinks he is. Although, he really wasn't my usual. The complete opposite. He was six-foot-one, nice body, absolutely gorgeous gluteus, seemed to have himself together and even a sense of humor. However, his head was inflated. I couldn't stand a man in love with himself more than anything or anyone else.

I grabbed my coat. Ray put a board over the broken window. The house was freezing. I turned on the heat and locked my doors, leaving behind a mess that used to be my home. *Out of all of the houses on the block why rob mine? My car is parked right out front. Did the burglar not think anyone was home? What a moron!* I'm no expert, but if you're going to break into someone's house, don't you think you should make sure no one is home?

As I walked behind Ray, the police cars began to scatter. I noticed that my car had a huge dent on the side as if someone had kicked it. My windshield was smashed and my lights were busted. I began thinking this was no random robbery. I looked toward the ambulance. A medium-sized fellow stepped from the ambulance with his head down. He wore a familiar coat, along with a familiar face. As I bent to get into my brother's car, I overheard one of the officers, "The paramedics say it's just a flesh wound, we can take him down to the station." I watched the officer as he handcuffed and pushed Jason's head into the squad car.

Detective Perry turned towards me and said, "What's wrong?"

I was embarrassed to say.

I can't believe Jason would do this. Is he crazy? I definitely wanted to go to the station to find out what the hell is wrong with this man. You dump people and you move on to find someone new. I know I was not caught up in some sort of drama. How far was Jason willing to go and why?

CHAPTER THREE

"Ms. Freeman, understand that we will try to do everything we can. But the extent of damage to your apartment might not be covered under the policy."

I began to fix my face, because the insurance man on the telephone was about to get blasted with words not too kind. "Mr. Tate, I pay every single month for that insurance policy, so I know you are not telling me you cannot fix any of the damages."

"Again, Ms. Freeman, we will have to get a look at the damages, total them up and see what we can fix and what you have to pay."

"What I have to pay! I pay a premium that covers my entertainment center, including my DVD player, television, computer, fax machine, all my furniture, broken windows, and my jewelry. So you get someone out here immediately!"

"Ms. Freeman, we will do everything we can."

"I know that's right," I said, closing the conversation.

It wasn't bad enough I had to come home to this zoo, but for someone to tell me they can't do anything about it, after all the money I pay for that policy. This was not the way to start off my week. Jason was insane. At the police station he began apologizing to me for what he had done. I didn't care for an apology. The maniac wrecked my place. I pressed full charges against him, and took out a restraining order. I just might have to get a dog too. A Pit Bull or Rottweiler will eat someone up. I don't even like dogs. But a woman has to do, what a woman has to do.

My place was a mess. My living room was turned up side down, my glass table was broken, and my dishes were broken. My pictures were smashed. My entertainment center was smoking. How could I have known how crazy Jason was? I broke it off with him a month ago. There was really nothing to break off. He was not my man. We didn't even sleep together. Yeah, he took me out, that was a given. He wasn't anything special.

I guess to him, what we had was real. I should have said, "Fuck off." On second thought, he would have probably dumped me in a garbage can somewhere if I were that abrupt. Nonetheless, he was tripping.

He smashed up my new VW Passat. I have to call the insurance agency about that. Lucky my pride and joy was in the garage. If he had touched my BMW 540, he wouldn't have made it to the police station. They would have had to read him his rights in a hospital bed.

He told the police that he just wanted to talk to me, but I wasn't home. Yeah right, if I am not home, dumb ass, you don't go banging up my place. He said he was upset that I didn't answer my phone when he called back. I checked my messages while at the police station and he left several messages. "Where are you, Sasha, I just want to talk, Sasha. Why you playing games, Sasha?" Plumb psycho, this was.

I should have known. There was some reason why I stopped talking to him. My mother always told me watch out for men if they are talking, "be my lady," after the first date or, "I love you," after the first week. I didn't pay much attention to Jason, so now my apartment paid the price. Luckily, Ray came home, and stopped him before he got upstairs. Jason must have thought I was with someone else for him to be tripping like this. Even though I was, Jason and I had nothing. He was not my man, so he had no cause to get upset if I was with someone else. I couldn't believe I was caught up in this fatal attraction. I mean, in my life there has been drama, but none ever hit this close to home.

The doorbell rang. "Girl, it is cold as shit out here let me in!" Lisa yelled from behind the door. She walked in shaking her head. "Girl, you told me he tore up shit, but damn, he beat you for your car too!" Lisa looked around the place, still shaking her head. She picked up what was left of the picture of all four of us, Me, Lisa, Tamieka and Michelle. Those were my girls. The ladies always into something and can never get out of it without drama. "Damn, homey, you don't got beef with us, why you going go mess up a perfect picture?" Lisa smiled. "Well at least you are alright; I didn't want to have to get 007 on his ass."

That was my girl; she always had my back through anything. Lisa and the other ladies were true friends. We had seen each other through some hard times. I closed the door as Lisa went on about how my place looked like a tornado.

I began picking up things because I wanted Lisa to shut up. "Well, I called you to help me, not bitch over my place."

"I know, girl, but I'm saying, he really did a number on you."

"Oh yeah, like Jake did on you."

Lisa retorted, "Oh, so now you want to get nasty with me. I'll just take my sorry ass out of here and let you clean this shit up yourself!"

That's how Lisa and I worked. We would go at it with each other. Many people didn't understand my friends and I, but that was okay they weren't one of us. I persuaded Lisa to stay and help me; she was going to anyway. And she just wanted someone to beg her.

"Girl, so what happened Sunday night? You left the club with Montel?" Lisa demanded information from me.

I knew she was going to bring it up, because I hadn't spoken to her since.

"I looked around and you were gone. Michelle and Tamieka told me you left with that fool! What the hell is wrong with you, Sasha? That boy has stomped and devoured your heart, and you have the audacity to leave with him! What's up with that? Are you lonely again? Who's next? Chris? Are you reclaiming all your old flames? Let me know, cause I..." Lisa went on and on like that damn Energizer bunny. She wouldn't stop.

My mind blocked her out as I went back in my head, going over what was said between Montel and me Sunday night. It had been years since Montel and I had talked and, as if nothing changed, I laughed with him, like I had never hated his guts. We were talking like that never happened. I wanted to forget about him, as if I ever could. I still loved him. Why? He treated me so bad.

The conversation began with me on the offense and Montel, as always, on the defense.

"What's wrong with me?" I said to Montel. "Why do I even speak to you? I can't lie to myself, I do want to be friends with you and be a part of your life. Its just, when I get close, I start to fall in love all over again. Every moment to myself I try to rationalize this feeling. Why can't I shake you? I soon realize that you can't rationalize this feeling of love. I feel like saying I don't know. Will I always love you and feel the same way about you? After we have moved on to separate lives, will we still feel the same way about each other? After it's all said and done, will we end up together, when we are old and gray? It's like I said, if it was meant to be, then it will be. I'll try to handle being friends. Can you handle it Montel?"

The alcohol in my system was making me jabber. I let most of my emotions out to this man and wanted him to do the same. "What, you have been listening to me talk for a while, now I want to hear what you have to say. Speak!"

"Excuse me that is no way to talk to, well, the love of your life."

I began to open my mouth but Montel placed his finger to my lips and spoke. "Shush, now I'm talking. Look, I love you; you know I'll always love you. You're a female me. I don't think I'll ever get rid of you, in my heart in my mind and definitely not in my soul. If I've hurt you in the past, I'm sorry. I'm man enough to admit, I have done some hurtful, things to you.

It's like I told you, I wasn't trying to get hurt. You knew the situation. I never lied to you about anything. Well, except, the way I felt about you—I don't know, I was scared, and confused. I didn't know if you wanted me as much as I wanted you. I thought you would leave me. I couldn't chance it. I already had security with my girl. You were like loose cannon. I didn't know what you were going to do next. My relationship was safe; I didn't want to be left with no one. I held on to both of you because I didn't know how to let you go.

I kept thinking about that one chance we had of being together. Do you know how much I want to get back to that time? But it didn't happen for a reason. It took me a couple of years to realize that was for the best. I would have only hurt you more and you would be even crazier.

On the real, I do love you to death. Doesn't matter what you do or where you go. I'm always going to love you. I don't want to hurt you. When I do hurtful things or say hurtful words, I am trying to protect you from me. I never ever want to hurt you, but you don't listen, you never have. When I see things aren't right or I have knowledge of how a situation is going to turn out, I try to get you as far away from me as possible. There were times when if things went down, different I knew you would never speak to me again. But, for what its worth I am sorry, and I hope we can be friends."

Montel said all I wanted to hear! Before I knew it I gave him a hug. I wanted to believe everything he said. I loved this man for so long. He was the only man I truly loved. He understood me and knew what I needed. When I stopped talking to him, a part of me drifted away. I thought I would never find love like that again. I would try to be friends with him and figure out what the next step between us should be.

Lisa still was rambling on. "Damn!" I said. "Will you shut your trap? It is too early to be overbearing. I know you didn't come over here to beat my head in about Montel!" I was annoyed with Lisa's disapproval.

"Sash, I'm saying, you could do…"

"I could do what? Better? Man, Lisa, you don't even know what you're talking about! Like it's any of your business, but nothing happened between Montel and me. We were in the car talking until 5 a.m."

"Talking and bumping like nobody's business—ha, ha!"

We both laughed.

Just think, Lisa and I had been friends for almost fifteen years. That is very unusual for girls like us to get along. I mean we used to get in so much trouble. We were both badass woman. Lisa took the D out of Diva. We both have butterscotch brown skin; we're talented, smart, witty, comical and damn right crazy. I can step in any room and the brothers are jocking. When Lisa steps in, all eyes center on her God-given down-to-her-roots behind. The stories we could tell, man! Lisa and I have a likeness to each other that has made us friends forever. Even when I moved off to college, we still kicked it when I came home.

Through these years apart, Lisa has been married, divorced, deported, audited and pregnant. Yet, she is still kicking. She just got her degree and is a social worker for Children's Hospital. Her five-year-old daughter is her world. And for a single mother, digging herself out of misery from a heartbreaking marriage, Ms. Lisa has got it going on. She's an award-winning mother, sometimes over doing it though. Like right now, trying to be my mother.

"Anyways, Lisa I will not repeat myself, Montel and I did not get intimate. So you can talk all the nonsense you want, it still would not draw my attention away from your hair."

"What you mean? You wish you could rock a Blondie, wit yo tired wrap, and give it up please!"

"Anyways, Lisa, where did the ladies end up going last night?"

"Please! Nowhere. Michelle went home to the kids and Tamieka; well you know who came to pick her up!"

"I know Linc didn't show up at the club."

"Yes he did, girl, Linc came into the club, T went out to speak with him, and she came back in an upset! Next thing I know we hear, 'Tamieka Williams, your ride is at the front.'"

"What! He did not page her in the club!"

"Yes he did, girl, T didn't even move. She kept sipping on her Amaretto sour, with no worry that her man was waiting outside."

"T is crazy. So she never got up?"

"Nope, not even when the DJ announced, 'Tamieka, you know you wrong. How can you leave a brother outside waiting in the cold?' Tamieka laughed, we all laughed, the whole club was laughing at Linc. T never went out there to see him. We stayed until around two in the morning. But wait a minute, when we got outside Linc was still there, waiting. Even though, T swore up and down she wasn't leaving with him, she got in the car with him and they drove off. I have to call her and find out what happened, I know he was pissed. You could see the steam coming out of his ears."

"T should not treat Linc that way," I said in Linc's defense.

"Try telling her that. T doesn't care. All the heartbreak she's been through, she needs a punching bag," Lisa said in Tamieka's defense.

I gave up and said, "Whatever!"

CHAPTER FOUR

Tamieka lay on her bed awake, wondering what she had done. Questioning what went on last night. She even had to question what had been going on for the past five years. It wasn't like T didn't love Linc. It was just the way he looked at her or called her name. As if she were the most beautiful and desirable woman in the world. Linc was a caring, sensitive man. He loved to do things for her. He quit his job in Atlanta and moved North just to be with her. Linc's salary wasn't much, but he pulled in extra money at his barbershop. He left his family and friends in Atlanta to share his life with T. You'd think that was enough for her to marry him after damn near eight proposals.

The last request T received for her hand in marriage was from another guy who almost ruined her. Maybe that's why her feelings for Linc were so in check. She didn't want to be hurt again. For a strong, family-oriented woman, it was hard to take a blow to her ego. T was completely devastated when she learned that Richard, her ex, was in love with another woman. T just knew that she would be with him forever. When he left, her whole world crumbled. Wedding invitations had to be sent back, money was spent to cancel halls, churches, flowers, everything. If it weren't for that high-paying salary, T would have been left broke. That wedding cost a fortune, not just financially, but emotionally as well. T had her entire future centered on that man. He was the reason she moved back to Boston, instead of starting a life in Chicago.

T picked herself up after about a year of rejected feelings of love and managed to save her business, but not her personal feelings of disgust in men. Then, Linc came along and turned T's world around. It would almost be a fairytale, if T could get her depressing heart to feel anything true for Linc.

Meanwhile the years piled on. T and Linc now lived in a false world, tainted by the reality that this would never work.

"Tamieka," Linc shouted, "Breakfast is served! I know you're probably hung over from last night, so I warmed you up some ginger ale."

"Oh, that's it," T said in disgust, "I thought I smelled eggs and bacon. It's just enough to make you nauseous."

"I made that for me, I thought you were sick from..."

"From what? Amaretto sours or you behaving like a stalker last night?"

A surprised look of bewilderment crossed Linc's face. "T, I only went to the club, because you said you were meeting me for dinner at Uno's."

"Linc, if I stood you up, have some dignity and go home. Don't come looking for me!" T sucked her teeth and rolled her eyes.

"Is it your time of the month or is it just a bad time?"

"No, Linc, I always have time for you to annoy me."

"That's more like it, I knew you loved me, T, it would just take time; like five years."

Tamieka got out of bed and moved towards Linc. "I know you're not trying to be the funny man in this, because I have got…"

"Oh yes, I know, plenty of other things to do with your time, than hang around a little man."

Tamieka got in Linc's face thinking, *what has gotten into him.*

"You know what, T, you're right. I'll just leave you alone for an hour, come back and maybe love you, but right now I just can't stand you!"

T thought, *has Linc finally gotten the picture? Did a light bulb come on inside his head? Does he finally realize that he's the fall guy and in a blink of disgust want nothing to do with me?* T watched her words and said "Maybe that is for the best right now."

Linc picked up his pride with that look of despair. He didn't want to hurt T. He just wanted her to stop bashing him. All he wanted was to love her and hope that one day she could return the favor. He got fed up for a minute and thought his abrupt approach would make T appreciate him more. He was wrong. "I'll try to call you later. I have a very busy schedule and I don't know when I'll have free time." Linc sounded defeated.

"That's okay honey," she said helping him out of the door. "Call me when you get a chance."

Linc looked like he was going to say something, like, I love you, but just kissed T on the cheek and left.

For a minute, T thought Linc was serious. He wasn't going anywhere. But the thought of him standing up to her did turn her on.

"Remind me never ever wear pumps or anything with heels to a show." Lisa exclaimed in agony.

"No one told you to wear that shit. You're twenty-eight years old, not nineteen. Can we please act like we know?" Tamieka scolded Lisa like she was a two year old. I swear, out of T, Lisa and Michelle, those two were always arguing.

"Always trying to be Ms. Cute," T added.

"T, now do not start with me, cause I might have to dig into your business, and I know no one is interested in that shit." Lisa always had a way with words.

"Don't start with me, Lisa, it's bad enough I have to deal with Linc's sorry ass. I came out tonight to have fun with the ladies."

"Whatever, hey Sash, why you so quiet?"

I rolled my eyes as I drove down the avenue, "Who said I was picking up Michelle? I am sick of this nonsense; we all have cars, why can't you guys meet me somewhere. I have to come all the..."

"Would you stop complaining? You are like a bitch on wheels sometimes," Lisa declared. "What happened, Montel didn't call you?"

"Wait a minute, did I miss a couple of days?" T interrupted.

I began thinking, *here we go all over again, I'll have to explain to T why I am speaking to Montel, she'll give me her unneeded two cents and we'll start arguing before we reach the show.*

"Sash, you didn't tell me you was messing with Montel. After the way he treated you? He broke your heart. I thought you learned your lesson?"

"Oh did you say something back there, T? I couldn't hear you; the music is up too loud," I turned up the music.

"You heard me, bitch, why are you putting yourself through this shit again?"

"Okay T, now you wonder why I didn't tell you, I knew what you were going to say because I have said it to myself. Montel and I are just friends. Damn."

"Just friends. If that were true, you wouldn't be upset that he didn't call you. Look, all I'm saying is that you're doing so well without him and you've been down this road one hundred times, so you know what's at the end of it," T declared.

"Thanks, but no thanks. I know what I'm doing. I'm an adult. Montel and I are just trying to fit each other into one another's life." I was trying to convince T and myself.

"Sash, what you need to realize is that there is and will never be a Montel and I. Just you and your idea of what true love is until you figure out you've been duped again."

"T, you are getting on my nerves now, just drop it, before I drop you off at the bus station."

"Drop me off! You're always quick to tell someone about what is wrong in his or her life, but you can't stand it if someone says something to you." T now had her arms crossed, eyebrows raised waiting for my response.

"Whatever!" I exclaimed.

"You know what? You can drop me off at a bus station. At least I know that I have been taken for a ride! Sash, you act simple sometimes, like you do not know what is really going on, like with Jason."

I stopped the car. "That's it bitch. Get out. Take the bus. You can no longer ride with us."

Lisa jumped in, "Chill out, Sash, chill out, T, this is supposed to be ladies night out."

"So what, T. I don't care. You cannot tell me shit. I know what I'm doing, and if it doesn't work out I'm one day wiser than the day before. Why do you care anyway? The real problem is not Montel and me. What's bugging you is that Ricky left you at the alter, and you hate any man who is not groveling or picking up the broken pieces of your heart." I increased the speed.

"Oh now you're silent back there, this conversation is not about me, it's about you and your unresolved feelings of man hating. You talk all this crap about other people's lives, but disregard the fucked up shit going on in your life."

Lisa held onto the dashboard, "Sash, slow down. T must have hit home because you are tripping."

"Whatever, T needs to mind her own fucking business."

T jumped in, "I am just trying to look out for you."

"T, I'm twenty-seven-years old going on twenty-eight, if I can't look out for myself then shame on me, right?"

"Whatever, You're tripping, Sash, and that is all you will hear out of me." T began to drink her Hennessey and coke.

The three of us pulled into Michelle's driveway. I honked the horn as usual. Michelle ran to the door and yelled, "Just a minute please, young ladies." She turned away from the door and ran upstairs.

"You kids it is time to get in the bed, Mommy has to go out for a little while."

Her oldest son Mitchell said, "Mommy you have to go to work again?"

"No baby Mommy needs to go out with her friends."

"Oh okay, I guess Mommy's need time off too."

"Yes they do, Mitchell", she said tucking him in tightly. She kissed his forehead and jumped down from the bottom bunk to kiss her youngest, Jamal.

He jumped up and said, "Have a good time Mommy and bring me something back"

"You, Jamal, can have anything, okay baby."

She kissed him and pulled the covers up tightly. She blew a kiss and turned off the light, just leaving a dim glow from their night-light.

Michelle rushed downstairs and left a little money for her mother for taking care of the kids. She knew her mother would watch them at no price, but she always felt like she had to give something.

That was just who Michelle was. No matter what direction her life was in she always gave much and expected little. I always thought life had left her with a feeling of gratitude. Even though money wasn't always in the bank, or men were not treating her the way she deserved, she could hold her own. Michelle was angelic in a way because her very presence just seemed protected or made you feel protected and looked after. She was the oldest out of all of us so of course we looked to her for advice and guidance. But she was more than a big sister type; she was our guardian, our guide.

Michelle's life was always in turmoil, but she always got through it. Her husband recently left her, so she has been a mother and a father to her children. She works two jobs and is still trying to go to school. Conveniently, her husband left her at a time when school and after-school programs kept the kids busy. Otherwise, I don't know what Michelle would do. Her mother was a big help and so were her sisters.

Of course, she had the ladies. Michelle has always been there for us. I could never see not helping her for all she has done for me. Michelle is not a voice of reason; she is a voice of reality. She let's you know how things really are compared to how you may perceive them. At times, it's done a lot of good for the ladies, but it never works for her. She can always tell you what is wrong with your life, but can never analyze herself truthfully.

Michelle remains in fantasyland when it comes to her husband. She still thinks he feels the same for her and that they are one big happy family. It's ironic because she can tell you immediately your faults but never admit her own, out loud anyway. Inside, she has got to know fact from fiction though. She cannot possibly be in denial. Maybe she can't cope with her own reality out loud. She can only deal with it inside and the reality is that Jamal left her for another woman.

Michelle knew of Jamal's extracurricular activities before they even got married. Maybe she tried to provide a home for her children so on the outside it looked good. As if her life was meant for television, Michelle played her part in the marriage and pretended that everything was okay. She knew that we were aware of all that had gone on in her life. However, she continued to delude herself, pretending that her family life was picture perfect, even if she knew otherwise. That was Michelle.

Her parents were the same way. She grew up with them together, but not. You would think that would have prepared her for what she really wanted from what she really had. In the end her parents divorced and moved on to separate lives, after Michelle moved out of their home at nineteen. Michelle is now on that road, but who can fault her for trying to make it work. She has a big forgiving heart. The flip side to that is her heart is to busy forgiving to recognize the pain of betrayal and hurt. She doesn't realize that she needs to forgive herself and love herself before her heart can do anything else. The ladies try to reason with her but no one can be the voice of Michelle's reality but her. In time, Michelle will come to terms with her part in her divorce. If she doesn't, she will continue to set herself up for a lifetime of denial and pain.

Michelle ran out of the house, waving for me to stop blowing the horn. She hopped into the back seat with Tamieka, smiling. "What's up ladies, you know I have to go to the ATM right!"

I began, "Oh for crying out loud, you're just stepped in here and you are already making demands."

"I didn't have time before," Michelle pleaded. "Anyways, I need to go. What's the attitude for Sasha?"

Lisa answered, "T and Sash got into it over Montel"

I interrupted, "Yes Lisa, go on tell the whole story, you have the habit of running your mouth"

"Damn, do you want us to drop you off somewhere, Sash, so you can handle your rage?"

I didn't respond and continued to drive straight to the club without stopping. As I pulled into the parking lot where the show was being held, my attention became focused.

Michelle exclaimed, "You didn't go to the ATM. I guess that means you are paying my way, Ms. MD."

While getting out of the car I said, "Stop your whining there's one inside the place."

Tamieka had not said a word since the argument. She looked like she wanted to apologize, but before she could; she noticed me walking up to this tall light-skinned brother who hugged me and gave me a kiss.

Tamieka said, "I thought this was ladies night out?"

I ignored her and let thoughts of why Montel was there fill my head. After all he hadn't called me like he said he would. He knew I was going to the show. Why go if he knows I will catch an attitude? As I remained hugging him like he was mine, I couldn't shake the feeling that this was not right.

CHAPTER FIVE

Okay, so Montel showed up at the concert that I told him I was going to. He didn't have a real excuse for not calling me though. He claimed that he was trying to get in touch with me all week. I thought *why didn't you leave a message. I have a cell phone, car phone and emergency pager; you couldn't call any of them?* Anyways, I pretended like everything was cool as we walked inside.

The concert was live. Jay-z, DMX, Mary J. Blige, Lil' Kim, Missy Elliot and the Da Brat, gave a dope-ass show. Tamieka was drunk off that Hennesey. I didn't know what she was going to say to Linc feeling as nice as she was. Michelle met Allan Iverson, as she was going to the bathroom. Lisa was still after DMX; I know she couldn't possibly be serious though. Anyways, I had backstage passes so we were chilling for a while.

I looked for Montel after the show, but couldn't spot him. He told me to wait for him by my car. That was an hour ago. The ladies were still inside trying to find the after party. I was down to go, but I wanted to see what was up with Montel first. I sat in my car in the parking lot for damn near an hour.

As the steam began to seep out of my ears, I noticed a tall gentleman walking my way. He was smooth from the way he walked, and his leather trench was open, probably so you could notice his Sean Jean suit. He came closer and closer to my car. I thought, *do I know you?* As he came from out of the shadows,

I frowned. It was Detective Perry. Damn was he following me or something?

"Ms. Freeman, I thought that was you, are you waiting for someone?"

"Hello, Detective Perry, no I'm not waiting for anyone. What are you doing here?"

"Just making sure everything is running smoothly, no altercations." He leaned against my car.

"I don't mean to be rude, but…"

"But what, Ms. Freeman, are you waiting for someone?"

I was now getting annoyed, "Look, Detective Perry, I appreciate…"

"Please, Sasha, call me Michael."

"Oh, so now we're on a first name basis? I never said you could call me Sasha."

"I figured, all we've gone through."

"Are you serious? Your character is wearing on me and my patience is weary. Shouldn't you be giving someone a ticket or something?"

Michael laughed. "I believe if I let you, you would insult me at any given moment."

"Well, you are starting to catch on finally."

"Yes, I am, Sasha. I am indeed."

"Did you want something or have something to tell me because if you don't…"

"Ms. Freeman, I came to tell you that Jason would not be bothering you any more."

"Thank you for that information."

"I'm not finished. He's in the hospital. Apparently, he was in a car wreck that looks self inflicted."

"What!" I thought, *I knew he was off but not that off.*

"He's critical. They don't know if he's going to make it or not."

"That's not good, what hospital is he in?"

"Why? You're not going to see him are you?"

"I don't know, a part of me feels responsible, but another part of me feels he didn't deserve that. He obviously needs help. I just want to send him a card or see if one of my colleagues could help him."

"The man trashes your apartment and you want to make sure he's all right. I guess I figured you wrong, Sasha. You're not a man-eater."

"Excuse me you need to stop talking to me as if you know me. I haven't even begun to say what I think of you, so back off. I just want to do the right thing."

"If that's all, I must say good night to you. I'll see you around, Sasha. Stay out of trouble."

As he walked away, I thought, *who the hell does he think he is? He has the audacity to criticize me? Is he crazy? Detective Perry or Michael, whoever the hell he thinks he is, better stay far away from me. How dare he call me a man-eater? If he only knew I was sitting out in the cold for a man who would never come.*

I got out of the car and began to walk inside the place to retrieve my friends. As I was walking, I heard someone yelling my name.

"Sasha, there you are, I've been looking for you."

"Montel, maybe you should have looked by my car where I said I was going to meet you."

"I did, but I saw you talking to some guy."

"Okay, so when he walked away, why didn't you come over? Or better yet, why didn't you meet me a hour ago like you said?"

Montel began his excuse, but it was all too familiar to me. I tried not to let him get to me but he could so easily. I couldn't show him I cared. He was the only guy who brought mush out of me. I would turn into a simple girl who needed direction. I wish I could block him out. *Someone save me, please, before I believe everything he says and leave with him instead of the girls.* As I tried to resist, Lisa came out of the concert looking for me. I flagged her and she came running over.

"What's up, Montel?" she blew out of one breath and with the other she began, "Sash, there is drama up in there, we were all back stage, and guess who came out of the wood work?"

"Who damn it?" I demanded.

"Ricky. You know Richard, stand-me-up-at-the-alter Richard."

My mouth dropped, "Where's T?"

"She's being escorted out by security as we speak."

"What happened?"

"Where should I begin? We were backstage, and I wanted to meet DMX, so T and I were looking for him. Michelle had gone off somewhere; you know how she wonders off. Anyways, we found DMX, but there was mad security around him like he wasn't going to talk to the fans. I thought that was odd because he always…"

I cut her off, "Lisa, damn it, would you get to the part about Ricky?" Lisa always got off the subject to talk about something that involved her, no matter what we were talking about.

Lisa began again, "Well anyways, T was already drunk so she walked up to one of the bodyguards and was like she wanted to meet DMX. Before the bodyguard could respond, T took a look to her left, she felt someone watching her. There he was all dazzled-upped with some groupie on his arm, Richard Dwight Masters." Lisa placed her hand on my shoulder to brace me for the next part of the story. "Before I could even say Hi to DMX, T was in Ricky's face shouting out all types of words. She was loud and very rude!"

"What did she say? She caused a scene?"

"Home girl stole the show. She asked him where the fuck has he been for five years, why wasn't he man enough to face her, why he couldn't tell her he didn't want to marry her, his brother had to. She called him a two-bit hustler who couldn't pay his bills. She told him she doesn't know why he has on a Versace suit, if his bills aren't paid. She called him a low life."

I interrupted, "What did he say?"

"Ricky was quiet as kept. He probably knew that if he opened his mouth, T would start throwing blows. I mean come on T is tall, stacked like pancakes, and no joke when it comes to beefing."

"If I were Ricky, I wouldn't say a word either. So what happened next?"

"Ricky knew his place with T, but the girl he was with did not. She began to open her mouth, somewhere in the lines of 'who the fuck are you?' Before she could finish her sentence, T landed her with a blow to the eye. If Ricky wasn't going to feel it, his date sure was. Then security had to step in, holding T back, and then Ricky wanted to speak. 'T, you always acting crazy, how could you hit my wife.' Both T's mouth and mine dropped. She said, 'Your what?' and charged at him. It took two full-sized security to hold her back. 'You married a tramp-looking, no-class hooker?' His wife should have never opened her mouth. I tried to calm T down, but a part of me didn't want to," Lisa explained. "She had every right to go off. She had not seen this man since their failed wedding day. He deserved everything he was getting, and that home wrecker did too."

"Where is T now?"

"Security has her, I think they're trying to hall her off to jail for disorderly conduct. After all, she was drunk in a public place."

"Where's Michelle?"

"Shit if I know. Probably looking for us or on that cell phone talking to, oh never mind you don't need to know that."

"Lisa, who is Michelle having a conversation with?"

Lisa backed up, "Probably her kids, yeah."

My voice heightened. "At damn near 12 a.m.? Come on, Lisa, spill it."

Just then security brought T out. They were prepared to put her in a squad car, but I saw a familiar face giving orders to the officers as usual.

I ran over to Detective Perry, hoping that our last encounter wouldn't affect his next decision. "Michael, can I talk to you for a minute please?" I batted my eyes.

"Not now, Sasha, I have to…"

"I know. That's my friend you're about to arrest. She doesn't need to go to jail, she just needs to go home and sleep it off."

"Oh, so now you want a favor from me. A minute ago you shooed me away like some pest. Is that how you treat all your men?"

Michael had the most audacious mouth. He would say just about anything to make me feel like a bad person. It's not my fault Jason is crazy or that guys just can't get enough of me. Who was he to criticize? I'm sure with his looks and his arrogance he had a trail of broken hearts lined up at his door.

"Michael," I said, trying to get past his comment, "This is not about me, this is about my friend. She didn't mean any harm; her emotions just got the best of her. Don't hall her off to jail like some criminal."

"Sasha, look, I wish I could help you but I can't."

I was now biting my lip, putting on my sad face. "I know you can help me Michael, you are in charge right?"

"Yeah, I am in charge but…"

"But what? You can't let her go with a warning? I'll make sure she gets home safely. You can even follow me."

Detective Perry began thinking it over. He signaled the officer to let T go, and then turned to me and said, "You're right this isn't about you, so don't even think for a minute that your charms work on me. I will let her go with a warning, but the person she assaulted is most likely to press charges."

"Oh, I wouldn't worry about that, Michael, besides I know you can make sure that doesn't happen."

As I walked away with my arm around T, I know Detective Perry saw me differently. The image of me being some self-righteous brat began to fade. He never dismissed my beauty, but was well aware of the trouble I could bring. He stopped starring at my rump in those fitted leather pants, and began to move the crowd away from the scene.

T said, "Thanks Sash, I want to apologize about before."

I removed my arm from around her neck. "Girl you know I know how you are. It's a given, you don't want to see me hurt I know, but I have to figure Montel out for myself. Kind of like you and Ricky, you finally let him have it. How did it feel?"

"It felt like a stone was lifted off my heart. He didn't even say anything. And that chick he was with was ugly. If that is the girl he left me for, I have to wonder what the hell is wrong with him. I look too good tonight for any man not to notice." T shook her hips.

We both laughed.

Michelle reappeared after talking to God knows whom. We all got into the car, but I stopped and thought Montel? "Hey, Lisa where did Montel go?"

"Girl, he left a long time ago, when you were talking to the police. He didn't need to stand around me. He knows I can't stand his ass."

We all laughed as I pulled away.

I thought *is he mad? Is he going to call me later?* I couldn't think, not with Lisa filling Michelle in about T and Ricky. T had a smile on her face from cheek to cheek.

I wished I could feel empowered like that about Montel. He had such a hold on me. I mean T hadn't seen Ricky for five long years. She went through hell without him. After he left her, she found out she was pregnant, but couldn't get a hold of him to tell him. All the stress of her hotel business going under and losing the one man she loved since high school took a toll on T's body. She lost the baby. I don't think anyone could ever get over the loss of a child. The timing just wasn't right for that angel to enter T's life. Ever since then, she's been working out hard at the gym; thinking that the next time her body will be able to take anything.

T and I are the only two out of the group who don't have kids, so we make up for it by spoiling Lisa and Michelle's kids. I don't know, somewhere down the road I want to have kids. I just want to find the right guy first, so my kids will not have to go through the absent- father drama.

Now T seemed content with the fact that she told Ricky off. I know it hurt like hell seeing him with another woman, his wife at that. A good thing she was drunk, cause if I know T, tears would have been falling from her maple-walnut face. She handled herself pretty well though. I just hope no one gets a hold of this story.

T is a successful owner of a chain of small hotels in Cape Cod. Her business associates would not appreciate seeing her knocking someone out like she was a title contender. Anyways,

I don't think T cared too much about that, she was just happy to have some sort of closure with Ricky. Or was this a beginning to unfinished business? God, I hope not. But I can't say anything; I am still dealing with Montel.

I dropped everyone off and since I lived the farthest I was going to stay at T's house. But I saw Linc's car in the driveway and changed my mind. As I was on my way home I checked my messages, "What's up beautiful, I haven't seen you all week, I hope you got your placed fixed, if you need any help call me." That was Damon; I didn't mean to ignore him. It's just been a crazy week. I liked Damon, we were cool. He always helped me out if I needed anything, a gentleman, and great in the sack. What's wrong with me? I better give him a call. After all, my body needs relaxation. As I pulled up to my driveway, a thought hit me, Montel did not call. I have got to stop stressing him. We agreed to be friends, that's it. He doesn't have to call me all the time, shit he hasn't called me at all actually. I will get it together one of these days, but today is not the day.

As my garage door opened, I drove inside to park the car. The garage door began to close and I turned around quickly because I noticed someone ducking into the garage. As he came out of the darkness, he grabbed my waist close to his body. "Where have you been woman?"

He began to kiss me, and undo my mink coat so he could fondle my breast. I kissed him back. The light in the garage went out. Damon picked me up around his waist and with his hand tapped my ass and said, "I missed you, where have you been hiding?"

I licked his lips with my tongue. "Don't talk. Bring me to that place you know I love."

Without a care in the world, Damon and I made love in the garage, on the steps leading to my apartment, and finally in my bedroom.

CHAPTER SIX

The weather was getting warmer and things were fresh and new. I love springtime. The air is not too hot or cold. It's the right time for new things, new people, new ideas, new events, new fashion and most of all new beginnings. I picked out the largest lobster in the grocery store for Damon to eat. I was planning a special dinner for him and me. Even though I had begun to see him less and less, I wanted to give him a special time. I had to tell him that this would be the last time he and I would be together. I was ready to get serious with Montel. My heart had finally healed and I felt confident about Montel's relationship and me. We had fallen back in love and now I just wanted to be with him.

When I met Damon it was a sexual attraction at first. I wanted him as much as he wanted me. I didn't know if he had broken up with someone or not, I just knew that I needed him at that time. I had just finished another unsuccessful relationship with some younger guy.

Yeah I went that route. I just wanted to pick up any pieces and meet a guy who would tell me, "Yeah, baby, wherever you go I'm going too, cause you're mine. You're so beautiful." That's what made me feel right at the time, some dude sweating me. But after that wore off, cause you done dropped the panties and are tired of picking them up with this same person, who you probably don't have anything in common with, you realize that is it. I don't need this any more.

That's how I met Damon. I just wanted someone to satisfy me in the bedroom. I needed a no-strings-attached type of relationship. Of course, men swear you are the only one they are with, but we women know the truth. A man can't just be with one woman until his appetite has been met, and that isn't until around his late forties or even older than that. Anyway I knew what Damon was to me.

When we met, I hesitated at first because I didn't want to seem needy or always on it, so I played hard to get. I explained to him that when you meet someone and you don't know anything about him or her, and you sleep together, you have just ended the relationship. You have no idea what is next after the sheets have been wet. You don't know this person and that person doesn't know you. Therefore, you get annoyed or lose interest very quickly. That person could be the most annoying person in the world, but you don't know that until after you have slept together. The person's personality determines how long that shit will last. That's how things went down with Damon.

I didn't want things to go that way with Montel, though. He and I had something special and I didn't want to end up in after-getting-the-booty mode. Meaning, Damon and I had reached the understanding that we just wanted to have sex. We could hold a conversation about our lives, nothing too personal though. We didn't have to lie to each other because feelings weren't involved and we knew this was not a relationship leading to marriage. We knew exactly what we both needed and we fulfilled that need. It's over now though. My need was met and Damon and I do not serve a purpose anymore.

Most of my time has been spent with Montel. He called me a week after the concert and met me for lunch at my job. The next week, we caught a show at the Comedy Connection. He started meeting me at my house after work, day or night. I flew with him to Los Angeles to promote this music group he was writing songs for. Montel and I started to grow again. He said things that made sense. He told me he wasn't ready then, and he'd be damned if he were going to lose me again.

When we first met I was sixteen, and he was nineteen. He was going to school in North Carolina where he could see different things and different people. I understood that. When he left for school, I told him I just wanted to be friends. He persisted, though. He started sending me applications to schools in North Carolina so we could be together. I wasn't trying to fall for it. Somewhere down the line I did.

I was seeing Chris, but my feelings for Montel grew. We could talk on the phone for hours running up everyone's phone bill. He wrote me letters of how he missed me and couldn't wait to see me. He would say how he wanted to be my first. I couldn't front, the thought of his yellow six-foot body on top of me turned me to fire. I wanted him then. I loved him then. He understood me, like no one else. He was the one for me, I thought.

I managed to make my way to his school in North Carolina during spring break of my junior year in high school. I was going to surprise him cause I was ready to do the do. Only the surprise was on me.

When I got to his school, I found his dorm room. I managed to walk by the residence assistant and look for room 109. The hallway was smelly, like a typical boys dorm. There were dudes in the hallway, girls in the hallway, radios playing. I walked to the door. There was a nice-looking boy who smiled at me as I knocked on the door. His smile turned to a surprised look, as if he knew me and knew what I was about to walk into. No one answered the door. I began to walk away, until I heard laughter and what sounded like a girl's voice. I opened an unlocked door to find Montel and some fake-weaved-out chick lying on top of him like she was riding a prize horse. My first reaction was to snatch her up and throw her and her weave out the window.

Montel jumped up, "Sasha? What? How the…yo what's up, cuz?" He winked at me, like I'd go along with this lie.

I gritted my teeth. "Cuz? Montel, what the fuck are you doing with this hoe?"

Before Montel could respond, this weave-o-matic girl charged at me, swinging. We began to thump around inside his room. I had been snatching weave for days as I gave numerous blows to her face. She was on top of me trying to choke me, as I kneed her. She bit me; the mark is still on my arm.

Montel got her off of me as the R.A. came running down the hall. The R.A. threw me out of the dorm. The girl was taken away by security and Montel was left to explain what happened.

Come to find out, he had been seeing that girl since he started school and was egging me on the entire time. He played me for a fool. I held feelings for him back in Boston while he was bumping with some chickenhead. True, I was seeing someone else. But I told Montel about Chris; he knew it wasn't serious. I cut Chris off the minute Montel told me he loved me. He was the one stressing that we should stay together. He had me filling out college applications so we could be together. He hurt me.

Slowly, I got over it. I resumed my relationship with Chris. He ended up being my first and the rest is history. I would never let any man influence me to do anything ever again. Decisions were left to me. It was all about my happiness.

Montel got kicked out of school because we were fighting in his room and the girl was talking about she was pregnant with Montel's baby. Historically, Black colleges do not play when it comes to matters like that. They are very strict about having girls in your dorm as freshman. The girl was lying about the pregnancy, however, and I heard Montel moved to New York to pursue a music career. Later, he wrote me apologizing.

I threw Chris in his face every chance I got. He invited me to come to one of his shows, but I resisted. Time passed and I went off to college, then med school, I moved, and didn't hear from Montel. I learned later that he had gotten with some chick he was seeing since high school. More information, I didn't know about. Montel was just playing the field. He could have been honest with me. I thought what we had was special. I tried to tuck away those feelings, but every guy I met I compared to Montel and became disinterested. Finally, when I knew where I stood with Montel, he popped back into my life, admitted all his wrongs and confessed that he just wanted to be with me. It took him all this time to realize I was the one for him. He couldn't deny it anymore. He was tired of living a lie.

Months went on as we spoke on the phone and hung out. Feelings came back as if they were never gone. Our relationship is more mature now and together we can handle anything. We have built a relationship that is very strong. He knows me. He always has. I sometimes believe it's fake because he's so right for me. We're two of a kind. He says all the right things and he's so honest with me. I sometimes am afraid that this could actually be because I don't want to get my hopes up.

Nonetheless, I've chosen to find out where Montel and I fit in each other's lives. Am I going to make a future with him or are we just supposed to be friends? Are we going to realize that we should never be anything? I have to know, I can't put it off any longer. We've taken little weekend breaks to hotels in New York and Rhode Island. We go shopping together and catch all types of shows. The past months have been wonderful. It's like we never separated. He's the same person I loved so long ago, and I finally am his. He loves me so much and he shows it.

As time went on, I realized it was time for me to make a decision; I was going to make a commitment to Montel. We talked about it and he lavished at the thought of us actually being together like that. We fooled around with thoughts of marriage and having children together. We were ready for the next step after dating.

Therefore, I had to stop seeing Damon like that. It would only complicate things and I really wanted to try to make it work with Montel. I have the tendency not to see things through. If you upset me once, you're not likely to get a second chance with me. I gave Montel a second chance, though. He was the only one. So here I was, ready for whatever was thrown our way. I was going to stick by him and be in his life forever.

After picking out the lobsters for Damon's special meal, I walked toward the checkout counter in the supermarket. Thoughts of the upcoming evening began to take place inside my mind. I had the scene all planned out. I'd tell Damon what was up and that would be that. He had left messages that I had returned days later. We saw each other less and less because between work and Montel, I had very little time.

Spending time with the girls also had to cut down. We hadn't hung out in a long time. Either one of them or I couldn't make a gathering or something. Our lives were going in all directions. I missed them, though. I spoke to Lisa and Tamieka Less. Michelle had drifted away from all of us at the time. I think it had something to do with her soon-to-be ex husband. I don't know. I guess things were going so good with Montel that I had not taken the time to see what was going on in their lives. That was selfish of me. Now that I have Montel I just want everyone to be as happy as me. I definitely have to get up with the girls soon.

The checkout counter line was always long so I picked up a magazine to peruse. As my attention began to point elsewhere, I noticed a little boy waving at me. It was Michelle's little boy, with Michelle. I know she saw me, so why didn't she say hello. If I hadn't glanced up, I probably would not have seen her. I waved. "Michelle, hellooooooo." I walked up to her. "Hey girl, are you going to walk by like you didn't see me?"

Michelle turned to me, "Oh, I didn't see you. How have you been?"

How have I been, I thought. Michelle looked worn out. Her hair was not together and she wore no makeup, except for the day-old eyeliner and mascara. She had socks over her lint-covered leggings with a dirty too-small t-shirt. Surprisingly the kids looked together. They wore jackets and boots and their jeans looked clean. What was Michelle's excuse? I heard through the grapevine that she and Jamal had gotten back together, but was he stressing her out that much? I tried to avoid saying anything, but I knew deep inside I had to address this hot issue. "Well, Chelle I'm trying to make dinner for this man, Damon. You remember him, right?"

"Oh that guy you sleep with from time to time?"

My faced turned ice. "What? Chelle, what is that all about? I know I haven't spoken to you in a minute, but you don't have to be rude."

"Look Sash, I know you and our friends don't approve of Jamal and me, but you don't have to talk behind my back about it."

"Talking behind your back? What, are we in high school?"

"If you have comments about Jamal and me getting back together, you should keep them to yourself. Your life is not so perfect. Just because you have a successful career as an obstetrician and own your home and what not, doesn't make you better than anybody else."

"Wait a minute, Chelle," I said, feeling defensive. "You are going down the wrong road, I never said anything about you and Jamal, and if I did, it would be to you. Don't get things twisted. This is why you have been avoiding me? You think I am going to give you grief about Jamal? Let me tell you something, Michelle, yes, I heard you were back with Jamal, but that is your business. I am not the one to criticize, but he did some foul shit. That is your life, if you feel me or anyone else is being harsh, I apologize, but you know that shit isn't cool. Once again, I am in no position to criticize. Let me refresh your memory though, we all give each other a hard time about everything. I'm still your girl. Anytime you need something I'm there. If you feel I give you a hard time about Jamal it's because I care what happens to you and I know you know you can do better. But, like always, no one listens; we can't run each other's lives. Shit, you guys are always putting your two cents about Montel or any other dude. Come on Michelle, I know you weren't avoiding me for that petty nonsense. What is up Michelle, for real?"

"I just needed time to myself to figure things out. Jamal and I have been married for a long time and I just want to give that a chance and see what our next move is. You guys don't understand. Every time I bring up his name all I hear is, 'that piece of shit, good for nothing.' I need to make my own opinion about him for myself. You just don't understand."

I began to think, *I do understand*. After all, I was doing the same thing with Montel. He and I have spent so much quiet time together that I had no time for anything else. I knew where Michelle was coming from. You need that time to yourself to figure how things are going to go without your friends dogging your man out.

"Michelle, I do understand what you're going through. I myself have been spending a lot of time with Montel exclusively. It has gotten to the point where I don't know what is going on with the ladies."

"Well, Lisa has a new man and T is on speaking terms with Ricky."

"In other words they're fucking," we said simultaneously.

"She's crazy," I said.

"See, there you go."

"My bad," I said as I slapped Michelle on her shoulder. "Oh please, Michelle, I know you were saying the same thing."

We both laughed.

"Michelle, I'm throwing a party for Raymond. He passed the test, so he is becoming a fireman."

"Oh that's good, is that what he wants to do with his life?"

"I think he wants to teach, but he's having issues. And he needs a stable income until he goes back to school and stuff. The party is not until next month, but I thought I'd tell you now. You can still put a call through. You don't have to act like a stranger and shit. We're your family, no matter what man is in your life and you don't ever forget that."

Michelle dropped her head, "I know y'all try to have my back. But I am grown and can take care of myself."

"I know Chelle; just keep your head up okay. I'll talk to you soon."

I left Michelle in the market. I understood where she was coming from, but still I couldn't stand to see her like that. She could do better and she knew it. I just wish she would stop living in fantasyland. If that wasn't bad enough, T was talking to Ricky again. I had to get up with the ladies real soon. Hell, I guess we all go back in time once or twice. Instead of new men, you repeat. Trying to see if things have changed or maybe you missed something. Maybe you just needed closure. You needed to close the door to old feelings that are still strong, thoughts of being with that person needed to end. Maybe we all needed that to truly move on. That was what Montel and I needed. He was a repeat. I just hoped that I didn't miss something from before and we were really meant to be together. This is something I had to know.

Of course I was running late, I had to let the steak marinate, boil the lobster and cut up a ton of vegetables. I was making a man-made meal. I had to do something nice for Damon. He and I had been kicking it for a minute, even though we both knew it was not going anywhere. Our season had ended and I wanted to start things off right with Montel.

As for Damon, I don't know what he wanted. He was a handsome young man, the kind of man that no one woman could hold. For some reason though, he thought he had to make me feel like I was the only one. I guess he thought that made me feel special. *Damon, who you kidding?* I laughed to myself. I knew very well what this relationship was about. The booty. There was nothing serious about it. Well, maybe the orgasms, but that's it. Don't get me wrong, I cared about him, but at the end of the day, I knew I was not going to be Mrs. Damon Harrin. He knew it too, even though he tried to front. We were not made for each other.

Never, under any circumstances, try to make your booty call, your man. It never works. I wasn't trying to play house with him or daydreaming about a future. The most daydreaming I did, was about the night before or the upcoming night. However, Damon did service me like I wanted, so I thought I would do something special for him, since this was our last time together.

As the food sizzled, I freshened up into one of my relaxing Victoria's Secret lingerie. Looking edible was called for tonight. It was almost time. I left the oven on, so the food would be warm. I started a fire and turned the slow music volume on low. I waited by the fire in my "ready-to-get-some gear" and sipped on my moet. The doorbell rang, I thought Damon was early. I sprayed the body mist on my neck, belly and between my legs. My hair was down, my face was natural, and my feet were bare. I opened the door with a look of essence to find Detective Perry at my door.

CHAPTER SEVEN

"What are you doing here? I'm expecting company."

Detective Perry said with a smirk, "Well I know we've only known each other for a few months, and I am handsome, but we should keep it formal."

He passed his way by me into my apartment trying not to let me see his facial expression. I turned him on; he knew it. But I was not going to let that keep me mute. "Well, just invite your rude ass in why don't ya. Look, I am expecting someone, not you. So you need to make your way back out this door."

"What's the matter Sasha? Afraid you might get caught in your mantrap."

"Listen here inflatable boy, I do not need nor want your comments today. State your purpose and leave. I don't care what you think. You don't count. You're just some nosy, smart-mouth, second-class detective who has nothing better to do than harass women you can't have." *Oh no, where did that come from, did I say that out loud? I can't let him get to me.*

The detective was silent for the first time since we met. He looked chipped, like I hit a soft spot. "Look, Sasha, I came over to tell you… well would you like to change first?"

"What? No! Can you make this quick?"

"That depends on your cooperation."

"What?" I was bewildered

"Is Raymond at home?"

"Raymond? What do you want with him?"

"Apparently, there have been some charges against him and I need to take him downtown. Since I know him, it would be best if I came to get him."

"What charges? Ray hasn't done anything!" I was always protective of my brother. I knew he was no angel, but I would stand up for him. After all it was only the two of us left. Our parents were killed in a plane crash twelve years ago, so I took on the responsibility of raising Raymond when I was onlysixteen. My mother's sister, Melinda, helped out as well. We stuck together because we were no good apart.

"Look Michael," I said, beginning to flirt, "I'm sure Ray-Ray has nothing to do with this, whatever the charge is."

"I know you want to protect your brother, but Tina Lewis is filing an assault charge against Raymond."

"Who? That scank trick that is properly being marked an X? She is trifling. Her word is no good."

"That may be, but she has bruises and black eyes that arouse attention and the attention is pointing Raymond's way."

"Tina's a liar. She's mad because Ray and her are finished and he has moved on. Let me tell you, Ray-Ray cut her loose two months ago when he caught her cheating with his friend, Marcus. After that he met Tasha. They've been kicking it since and Tasha is pregnant. Ray and her are now trying to do right by their baby. Anyways, Tina hates on Tasha, because Tina still be messing with Marcus, who is Tasha's cousin's man. Did I lose you Michael?"

"No, I know what you're saying. But regardless, Ray should not be putting a hand on Tina."

"Okay, you are not listening. Tina is a liar. Whatever, Ray and Tasha are in New York telling her parents about the baby. So as soon as he gets in, I will have him go to the station and make a statement."

"How do I know you are not making this up?"

"Why would I lie?"

"To protect your brother."

"Look, he is not here, you can check, but you can't stay…"

"I know you're expecting someone."

"Right, so see your way out please."

"I hope for your brother's sake what you're saying is true. Ray could be in a lot of trouble if this isn't straightened out."

"Yeah, I got this DT. Can you go now?"

"I'll go, but I'll be back if need be. And try to have some clothes on next time."

I swung at him, but he blocked my fist and pulled me close to him. We stood for a second. Michael's mouth began to open as he came closer to my face. I closed my eyes and puckered my lips, as Michael said, "Next time don't over-use the body mist. You could give a brother an allergy attack."

I sucked my teeth and pulled away. For a second Michael caught my attention, but I should have known better.

Michael left. It began to get late. Damon was fifty minutes late. Now, he really wasn't getting any. Just as I made my way to blow out the candles, the doorbell rang.

"Well ,Damon, nice of you to join me."

Damon scooped me up and kissed me softly. "How's my baby doing?"

"Damon, you're late, which means I have an attitude."

"Well, I hope your attitude changes, cause I have been missing you all week."

"Whatever, sit down we have to talk. Damon, I know where you and I are heading."

Damon, interrupted, "You know I am not ready for anything serious. In fact, I'm seeing someone right now and I wanted to tell you that we could still kick it. I know you always said to be honest, so I am being honest. Before there was no one else, we were just kicking it. Now I feel like I need to let you know about the other woman."

"Whoa, whoa, Damon, this is not how things are supposed to go. I have to let you know that…"

"I'm saying you and me can still kick it. I'm not giving up our late nights for no one, but I care about you and I want things to be open between us."

I thought *so much for feeling special.* Damon rambled on about his new revelation of how he enjoys our platonic relationship. He had no clue that I wasn't down for a continuance of this. I was the network canceling this show. He wasn't going to diss me. I hold the cards. We can still kick it? Translation: we can still have sex! Oh, hell no that episode was over. No reruns! I sipped my Moet and tried to pick and choose my words as Damon scuffed down his meal. "You like the food?"

Damon just nodded.

"Well baby, it seems we both have gone shopping."

"What do you mean?"

"I am seeing someone else as well."

Damon stopped eating.

I snickered. "Only difference is I want to get serious." With him of course. Because like you said, you're not ready for anything serious. So here's the deal, this is our last night together. We cannot continue late evenings or early mornings. We definitely can't kick it or be platonic. So I'm glad you met someone, cause I cannot be with you like that anymore."

Damon began to drink his wine. "So you're saying no more whipped cream and handcuffs?"

"Not unless you're eating a pie or being arrested." I burst out in laughs.

Damon stood up, "That's not funny, Sasha. Damn, that is fucked up." He walked away from the table.

I followed him and playfully put my hands on his back. "Come on Damon, you knew our situation, don't front. There was no relationship here, just physical satisfaction. We are not moving in together, getting engaged or having any children. You know this was fun. You were what I needed at the time. Now my needs have changed, but you haven't. Meaning, it's time to let go and move on. We've exhausted the possibilities."

Damon turned around. "I know you were trying to gas a sister's head up, but I knew from the start what we were to each other." He put his arms around me and kissed my lips. "Does he kiss you like this, touch you like this or even hold you like this?" He began to kiss my neck, then my chest, navel and thighs. "Answer me, Sasha!" he said as he picked me up.

I tried to resist that tingle between my legs. "Damon" I said softly. He sshhed me as my legs wrapped around his waist. I bit his lips. "Damon, baby, I lust you, but I love him. In time, when you meet the one, you'll know the difference and want love any day over lust."

Damon tried to let my words sink in, but he continued to kiss my body. Clothes were pulled off and we lay naked, wrapped in each other's arms, giving into lust. I got a blanket and blew out the candles. I knew that this was it. Damon and I could not give way to each other's physical desire any longer.

Damon, left the next morning, knowing what last night meant. I slept late that morning, closing the world out, feeling settled because I knew where I wanted to go and with whom. I felt optimistic for a future with Montel. I shut out all doubt and insecurity felt before.

CHAPTER EIGHT

Saturday. I had'nt seen a Saturday free of work in a month. I was looking forward to this day. Since the ladies and I had lost touch we were going to spend this weekend together, just us girls. It was Memorial Day weekend and May had hit an all time high of eighty-eight degrees. Such a weekend could not go unnoticed. Of course, I would have loved to spend the weekend with Montel, but friends are important and Montel and I had been spending all the time possible together. We needed a break. I couldn't believe I was in a relationship exclusively. I got rid of all my flames; I threw out my phone book, and all my sheets. Pictures were tossed to the attic, and everything else from past relationships. They were out of sight and out of mind. I was in love, not puppy teenage love, but real love. The kind of love that Mary J Blige sings about. A love that was so unbelievably true. I finally found my soul mate. I knew that in time, I would not be able to hide from it, and it would not be concealed from me. Montel was everything I wanted in a man. He was intelligent, handsome, funny, devoted, strong, and easy to talk to. He knew what he wanted out of life and did it. We just connected like that. I could tell him anything and he would understand. I knew it was meant to be.

The plan for ladies weekend was this: Saturday morning would be dedicated to being pampered at a spa. Nails, feet, back rubs, the whole nine. After that shopping, something I enjoyed doing by myself. But sometimes you got to have the ladies along. Then Lisa and Michelle would pick up the kids from swimming lessons at the YMCA and we would trot off to the Cape. T had us staying in one of her cottages on the Vineyard. I rented a Suburban, so we could leave together. Lesson one when rolling with females, leave together, because females will make you late. The whole weekend was dedicated to us hanging out, like we used to.

I heard about T and Michelle's turn-backs, but I knew little about this new man Lisa was seeing. I didn't know his name, but I heard he was really nice to Lisa's daughter. This could only mean he planned to stick around. Now that is a different story. Men who involve themselves with other people's children always have a plan. In Lisa's case, I hope he only had good intentions. Lisa had been through so much in the past couple of years.

When I went off to school, things just were not fun any more for Lisa. She got married to some jerk from Jamaica. I didn't even attend the wedding because I told her she was stupid. Lisa could have gone to school, or done anything with her life. I remember she called me at school to tell me of the union. She was tired and she wanted someone to take care of her. School wasn't her thing. So she met up with this fool, Jake, and he married her, took her off to Jamaica and that was that. She sent me postcards and called every once and a while. Soon, I heard from her less and less.

Finally when I came home after my sophomore year at school, Lisa was home too. Not with Jake though. Just an oversized belly, a couple of bruises and a tear-breaking story. Bottom line, Jake fucked up her life. He was pushing drugs. He had a smooth operation, but apparently not smooth enough because the FBI caught up to him. On top of that he had another wife and child in Atlanta who were mules in his operation. Lisa was locked up, too, for being an accessory. She was in a federal prison for months, pregnant, with all her rights stripped from her. Luckily, they realized she knew nothing, and could not help them bring any of Jake's partners down. She was living lavishly in Jamaica with a big house, a Mercedes, diamonds and a maid.

After the bust, she couldn't go back to Jamaica for fear of her life. She ended up here. She set up a nice home with money she kept secret from Jake. She wasn't working while she was pregnant either. One week after she delivered her daughter, the IRS said she was living beyond her means. The house, the car, everything was auctioned off and Lisa was left homeless with a brand new baby. The feds had something to do with that I am sure. Nonetheless, Lisa, with no money, no man, not a pot to piss in, made it.

Anyway the past is the past. I can't wait to see what the ladies are up to. This was sure to be a fun weekend.

Montel rolled over and silenced the beeping alarm clock. "Baby, don't you got that thing to do today with your friends?"

He listened to me all the time. I let out a yawn. I had already been up since 6 a.m., just thinking about how happy I was and my plans for the day. Montel had been spending the night at my house for the last four Fridays. I loved being around him and he couldn't get enough of me. "What you trying to get rid of me?" I said as I shifted my pelvis his way wearing nothing but a tank top and panties.

"Never that, Boo, I'm just wondering if I am going to get fed today or do I have to starve. You know I like the way you do it up in the kitchen, so why not hook a brother up baby?" Montel began to kiss my forehead, then my neck as he let out a sensual grunt. "See that's the sweetness, I'm talking about. What's up?"

I moved my eyes downward, signaling Montel to follow. I began in my sexy voice, "Yeah, that is what's up honey, don't stop what you were doing, come on finish."

Montel placed the back of his hand on my cheek, "Come on, you know there's more to us than that. In time you won't be able to get enough of me."

My mind understood what he was trying to say, but my desire within just couldn't. He got up and I followed. He led me by the hand toward the stairway to go downstairs toward the kitchen. I jumped on his back, wrestling him to the floor. My five foot frame couldn't hold him, he pulled back landing on the bed with me under him. Montel then turned around as he lay on top of me and he began to kiss me. My hormones raced as I spread my legs wide and ready. Then Montel stopped. *Is he serious?* I had to get up before I got evil. I felt like the dude pleading to get some virgin girl to do it with him.

Montel said, "You always playing, Sasha, you can't wrestle me, you too little, give it up."

I mashed his face playfully. "Whatever, be stingy if you want to. I don't know why you always over here on Friday night. What happened, the wife kicked you out again?"

Montel rolled his eyes, "Yeah, she decided to replace me with your man. You know that Black cop, that bad boy wannabe."

I was confused. I knew he wasn't talking about Michael. That inbred was the farthest man from my mind. "Oh, so now you got jokes stingy?"

"Yeah okay, you know you're mine, and you know you want me over here, no matter what we do."

That was the truth, but I couldn't let him know that, I was still a bad ass, he couldn't tame me, and so I thought. "Why you worried about Michael? You trying to mark your turf?"

"You didn't hear me, I am not worried. I got you." Montel began to hum, *The Roots* featuring Erykah Badu, "*If you are worried 'bout where, I been or who I saw, baby don't worry you know that I got you.*" He began to kiss my lips.

"Don't finish what you can't start," I said obnoxiously.

Montel snapped at me, "What, is that all you about?"

Sexually frustrated, I said, "You know what, you are becoming way to sensitive about this. How old are you now? Look, you can't sit there and tell me you don't want to, cause I see it in your eyes. You're teasing me. Why, I don't know. Yeah, we talked about it and talked about it, and so forth. We're both adults and ain't neither one of us virgins. There has been plenty opportunity, and we've known each other for years. What is the problem? You sleeping with someone else?"

This was a thought I tried to keep to myself, I didn't want to let my insecurities show, but Montel was being difficult.

He stood silent for a minute. Then he pulled me next to him and sat me on his lap, like he was Santa Claus about to grant me my Christmas wish. "Look Sash, I know you, true, you know me. But, what we have is very special to me and I don't want anything to go wrong. When we're together like that I want it to be special, because I've wanted to be with you for a long time. I'm waiting until the time is right. It's not just about sex when it comes to you. I love you; you know that. And no, there's no one in my life but you. You're the only one who could hold me down. That's why I am waiting. You're that special."

I took in what he was saying, but still wasn't getting it. That speech could only last for so long until my mind started clicking to what was really going on here. But, I took it in, just like I took in all that he said. See when you are in love, things make sense, and if they don't they will. You just don't worry about it. The truth was Montel had me snowed. I would do anything for this man. My blinders were on and my head was buried deep under Montel's hypnotic snow bank. We were in love, and that is how love went.

I kissed his forehead and said playfully, "Since you ain't heating up things upstairs, how about you satisfy my other hunger?"

Montel smiled, as he carried me like I was his child, downstairs. He hugged me close. I wrapped my legs and arms around him so he couldn't let go. He didn't though, he watched his every step, so not to let me fall. I buried my head into his shoulder as he carried me into the kitchen. After, eggs, bacon, home fries and toast, Montel, ran my bath water. He filled it up with bubbles and even scrubbed my back.

I said with a smile, “Keep this up and I might not need to go to the spa.”

He giggled, I giggled and that was that.

CHAPTER NINE

Montel blew me a kiss and drove my BMW from the car rental place, as I drove off in the White Suburban I rented to meet the ladies. The events were set in motion for the day. I met up with the ladies and we got our nails and feet done. Gossip in the spa amongst us began to start just like a regular day. We couldn't all go to the salon to get our hair done because that would take an entire day. I wore mine in a ponytail, Lisa had her Blondie shortcut already done yesterday, T wore her hair down and Michelle had synthetic braids.

Lisa always started the issues. "Hey Sasha, what's up with Ray-Ray's girl, Tina? I saw her at my clinic the other day for battered women."

"Oh please, that hoe has not been battered, well not by Ray anyways. She's tripping because Ray-Ray's with Tasha and they're about to have a baby, so she's acting a fool. You know, kind of like how T was at the show."

They started laughing.

"Whatever," T interrupted, "when a man stomps on a woman's heart, he should expect repercussions."

"T, I'm saying, to take it so far as to getting the law involved, that is some cowardly crap," I said.

"Well, nothing's worse then a woman scorned, everyone knows that. And don't let no other woman get involved, she is in for torture," T stated.

"Montel and I started off kind of like that back in the day. He was seeing someone, I didn't know at first, but when I found out, I was bugging. Cutting off pagers that were in my name, calling his house and hanging up, leaving silly messages on his answering machine. It got to the point where I wanted to confront the girl. But, if there is one thing I will never do, it's call up another female and talk about stay away from my man. That is childish, because first of all, he most definitely didn't tell you about her, so he hasn't said shit to her about you. Accusations are a different story. You start throwing out her being the sidekick, and then she flips it on you, like that is my man, and name calling starts. Next thing you know, you're saying 'where you live, I am about to come down there and beat your ass.' She's saying, 'ask your man where I stay, come and get some bitch.' You rallied up, don't know if this chick got pots and pans waiting for your ass, go down to her house with like ten girls, four are ready to fight, and that bitch got the whole projects waiting for that ass. You never realize, until you're through with the boy, that he had you fighting over him while he is sexing the next chick."

Lisa started laughing. "You bringing back memories, girl."

T, cut in, "Sash always bringing up old shit, and finding some way to talk about Montel too." T and Michelle gave each other dap, while they hollered.

"Don't hate, Montel and I are in love."

They started laughing.

T said, "You know where love takes you, stop fronting, forget love, get the money, the house, the cars and the ding a ling."

"T, you really don't believe that do you?" I questioned.

"Anyway, those days were good to me, when we were younger. We were naïve, no clue to the real world, just me, myself and some good sex and a bottle of deuce/deuce Old English to go with it," T said.

"You stupid, T," Lisa cut in. "I wouldn't trade them days for no one. But we were stupid, fighting over dudes. I never fought over any man, though."

"Yeah right," T stared at Lisa like, yes, I am talking to you. "We all use to be hood rats, baggy clothes, triple goosed down, skullies, carrying army knifes in our boots, rolling ten deep to the movies, rolling with the fellas. We thought we were the bomb."

"True, but I never got into a beef over no dude," Lisa declared.

"Me neither," I agreed. "It wasn't worth it, I knew he was to blame and I was gonna handle him."

T and Michelle looked at each other like *yeah right*. They all started laughing.

T said, "Sasha, what about KeKe and Mika, the twins you fought over Chris's corny ass. Lisa, what about Hilda that big giant from the bricks?"

"Oh yeah," Lisa reminisced. "That wasn't my fault she came charging. I didn't know Malik was messing with her."

"He was messing with you both," T added.

I corrected them, "Nah, Hilda liked him, and he wasn't interested."

"So she thought beating my ass would make him not want me. Little did she know he had my back and stomped his size eight in her ass for messing with me," Lisa said.

"Yeah, Malik was cool," I said.

It took Lisa a long time to get over his death. Till this day, I will never figure out why dudes still are killing each other over their block or their respect or whatever. I guess, since I don't live that life, I don't understand. The ladies fell silent for a moment.

Trying to change the subject, I said, "Well Lisa, keep a heads up on that Tina chick, make sure her story is legit because I know Raymond didn't have nothing to do with that."

"I'm way ahead of you, Sash. I already signed her up under my counsel."

"Yeah, cause you a nosy gal, Lisa."

"Whatever! I don't gossip. I just share information."

We started laughing again.

Michelle said, "It is messed up how far sistas are willing to go these days over some dude. Back then we were ready to fight, but now-a-days chicks are on some other type mess. It's one thing to be messing with someone's boyfriend, but breaking up happy homes, black mailing men for money, even sex. Do this, or I will tell your wife, do this, or she will get a phone call. I know that's how it was with Jamal."

Silence took over. Michelle never gave up any info on Jamal and her, not to all of us at once anyways. She kept her life private when it came to Jamal. No one knew what to say. This was such a sensitive topic.

I said, "Jamal's girls would blackmail him to stay with them?" As if I could believe it.

"Yeah, this last one, Tammy, he told me she would beat him out of his check or force him to have sex with her or she would tell me that they were having an affair."

You believe that bullshit. It was true. Michelle had gone completely deaf, dumb and blind. She was under his spell. A man like Jamal doesn't have to be forced to have sex. He was a dog. Secondly, he had to come up with an excuse of why he was giving this chick money. Blackmail my ass, this I am sure wasn't Jamal's first affair that Michelle knew about, so why would he give a flying fuck, if Michelle knew or not. Jamal knew exactly what to say to Michelle to get that door back open. Maybe if I egged Michelle on she would realize how stupid this sounded out loud.

I said, "So that is why he left you for her?"

Michelle said with enthusiasm, as if she had me sucked into this story, "Yeah he didn't want to hurt me or the kids, and he couldn't afford nor stand this blackmail anymore, so he thought it would be best to leave me and finish what he started with her, so she couldn't blackmail him anymore."

I tried to hold in my laughter with this next comment I made, "So he left you cause he didn't want to be blackmailed anymore?"

Lisa and T turned away or tried not to focus on Michelle, cause they both were hip to all his bullshit.

"Yeah," Michelle said looking for sympathy.

T busted out, "Well I guess it worked cause he's back at home blackmail free."

Who was Michelle kidding? We knew far too well about Jamal. But I guess since we were outsiders looking in on the situation, we could see what Michelle couldn't.

Lisa quickly changed the focus, "Women don't play now. We get the money and half on everything you own chump!" She slapped T's hand and said, "As you get older, things change, needs change. Forget about fighting to keep a man, you can have him, just send all the other assets my way."

We all started laughing.

T said, "Linc pays for everything, and he is over."

I interrupted, "But T, Linc has not done you wrong."

"So what! He's a man, and a man eventually turns back into a little boy, because he always has been. Afterwards the moon comes out and he turns into a vampire out to suck all he can out of you."

T's vivid look on relationships had me scared. Now I have been through some hard times with men, but the number Ricky had done on T was frightening. She hated men, even the good ones like Linc. I chose my words carefully with T. "Well, T, it has been five years, Linc hasn't showed his colors yet. I think you have seen all there is to see."

"Nah, he hasn't shown them, he wants me all to himself, so he tries to butter me up, so I will give into him. But I won't, ever. Love is wasted on men you are in love with. When you love to be loved, you are punished. When you love to get what you want you come out smelling like roses."

Again, T and Lisa gave each other dap. Now Lisa, true, has been through the mud, but she couldn't possibly share T's outlook on men and relationships. From what I could see Linc's love for T was genuine and he would do anything for her. T just didn't know how good she had it. Love was loving her, she just didn't know it. Anyway, I couldn't win with T so I changed the subject. "Lisa, heard you got a new friend."

"Yeah," Lisa smiled. "He treats me well these days."

"D, that's his name?"

"That's what I call him, D honey, D money, and D dick."

We laughed.

"Damn, Lisa, he got any friends. I gots to have one of those," T shouted.

I looked at her, "Don't you have enough on your plate?"

"Sasha is all content with Milk dud, and Michelle, well she's married, so I need a smile too."

"What about Ricky?" Lisa asked.

"Yeah," I agreed.

"Ricky who? I'm just stringing him along, like he did me, breaking him off a piece to get back at that bitch wife and teach them both a lesson. Teach that wifey of his how it feels to be polishing a knob that is diving head first in another woman's pootang."

We all laughed except Michelle. Of course she didn't agree with T's antics. "Do you ever think about how that affects his home? I mean that woman is constantly checking messages, phone bills, laundry. She's practically glued to his side any and everywhere they go because she can't trust him. That isn't funny, T. The only thing that teaches you is how not to trust men or yourself. You become a spy on his every move, checking body parts, smelling his penis, and smelling his clothes. You start to wonder if his disinterest in sex or him coming so quick is due to the stress of work or is he being satisfied somewhere else on a regular basis? Your mind is always wondering"

"Damn, Michelle," T cut in, "I'm not worried about her cause she wasn't worried about me when I was at the alter and they was in Tijuana somewhere sipping on Pina Coladas. As far as trust, you wouldn't need to play spy if you did trust him. All that shit you talking is to each his own. Meaning, if you don't trust Jamal, deal with it. Let him go or live this crazy life that you are living."

Michelle stood up.

The Chinese lady, said, "Wait, I am not done with your toes, you pay now!"

Michelle didn't even hear her, she needed some air. T had said what we all were thinking but didn't want to hurt Michelle's feelings.

Lisa and I looked at T, *damn did you have to say it?* She knew what she had done, and let the lady finish her pedicure. She paid for herself and Michelle and proceeded outside to redeem herself with Michelle.

The funny thing was that T had been in that same situation. She played detective with Ricky, come to think of it, we all had the trust issue one time or another with men. T knew of Ricky's activities but chose to ignore them. She followed along with him hanging on his every word. She forced the issue of marriage. He went along with it until the day of the ceremony. Knowing he didn't want to get married, T went along with it. I guess she finally realized it when she didn't have a groom meeting her at the altar. She had been in a relationship where love was one sided. She loved him but he only loved himself. She was the giver and he was the taker. Now she is taking it all, while Linc continues to give it all away. That is how those relationships worked. At one point in time you expect the tables to turn, so you wait until you just accept it or grow enough strength to move on. T, I thought, moved past Ricky, but slowly and steadily she was being sucked back in, no matter what she said her real motives were.

T and Michelle made up and we proceeded to the mall. Shopping came like second nature to me. After spending some change, Michelle and Lisa picked up their kids, we loaded the car and off we were to what looked like a promising getaway.

CHAPTER TEN

Lisa's daughter, Jasmine, loved the pool; Little Jamal and Mitchell dunked each other's heads under the water. The chlorine water darkened their chocolate bodies and made their skin ashy. The sun beamed all day as the kids enjoyed the water and the ladies relaxed, chilling like we didn't have a care or responsibility in the world. The day turned dim as Lisa and Michelle prepared the kids for dinner and then bed. T had been drinking already, getting an early start for the evening.

This was a good idea, I thought Everyone was relaxed, having a good time. The kids enjoyed this outing so much a thought fell through my head about kids. I wanted at least three, but first I would need a donor. Montel and I had talked about kids. He wanted a boy, of course. I preferred all girls, but one boy would do, like Ray-Ray and me.

Our parents were together. They married young, had us young, and died young. Our Aunt Melinda got us through that. She took us in and her daughter, Tanya, became like a sister. Auntie Mimi, we called her, wasn't married though. Her husband had left, like a lot of dads. That generation was weird like that.

See the way I see it is, our grandparents knew what the institution of marriage was about. They stayed together no matter what. Our parents were too liberal. If things weren't working, the marriage was over. Now look at us today, my generation is the worst. Marriage is much later in life like thirty and up. If you are married, you're having an affair. Others are engaged with kids and a ring that signifies one of these days they will marry. But not any time soon. I don't want it to be like that. When I get married and have children, I want a family. None of this father-some-of-the-time bullshit. However you are a product of your environment. If your parents weren't together growing up, you see that as okay and not a problem. Single parenting is okay, you think. Well, both my parents were together, so that is how I want it.

Even though Aunt Mimi wasn't following that path, she held us down growing up. She was cool. I could talk to her about anything, anytime. She never tried to replace my mother; she became more of a close friend. Tanya and I hung out all the time. She was a little older, but she let me tag along with her crew until I met the ladies. Tanya got married two years ago, so we don't hang out as much any more. I have to make a mental note to call them when I get back. I haven't spoken to them in so long. Anyways, children I looked forward to having.

Michelle made potato salad and T started the grill. It would be getting dark soon, so we wanted to hurry up, feed the kids and put them to sleep to let the party begin. Time to break out the wine glasses, cards and what not. T brought some smokes. I tried to resist but what the hell. I will just drink some vinegar in case the job comes up with a surprise urine test.

The first time I ever puffed lah was with my cousin Tanya and her girls. Once you smoke you don't know what the hell you're doing, so getting high didn't feel like getting high until the second time around. I was sixteen, smoking and drinking, not a care in the world. When you start young, by the time you are my age your tolerance decreases and hard drinks turn into soft mixed drinks like Amoretto Sours. T started rolling the blunt, I started mixing the daiquiris, and Lisa popped open the Moet. We started drinking and running our mouths as usual. We decided to play questions, this drinking game, you could ask anyone a question, but they couldn't answer, they would have to ask someone else a question. We played until we got dizzy. After the alcohol took over, other questions that weren't part of the game arose.

"So, Sash, I'm saying you and Monty haven't hit the sheets yet?" T said, "Whazzup with that?"

I said defensively, "We just haven't had a chance. A relationship can be based on more than just sex."

T busted out laughing, "Who you kidding Sash? Sex is like food to you. Shit, it's like food to anyone who isn't fronting. We pretend it's the men who want it all the time, but it's really us. We're just holding out. So let me understand something, Montel is holding out? Are you sure he's a man? Cause I know you, and you aren't holding anything out, you want it bad. What is the issue? Oh his thing is too small?"

"Yo! T, chill. Montel and I are each other's business. That's why I can't tell you guys nothing, you always up a sister's back."

"Whatever, you be acting the same way when shit doesn't sound right."

I was annoyed with T's drunken ass, "What, there can't be a relationship without sex?"

"Yeah, maybe when you're a virgin or just young like in elementary or middle school. But that isn't the case here. Kids now days are having sex at that age anyway."

"See what I mean, T, kids that young shouldn't be having sex? Where are there parents?"

"Oh don't get high and mighty on me. You been sexing since high school, stop trying to change the subject, I am talking about two adults."

"T, you been sexing since you were twelve. And?"

"I'm saying open your eyes. Montel and you aren't virgins, so what the hell is up with that?"

"There comes a time in everyone's life when you just have to mind your own business. We have come to an age where things are better left unsaid. Montel and I, are Montel and I, and that is it."

"All I am saying is, if you two are so much in love what is the issue? Something doesn't sound right, and that is all I am going to say about that."

I wanted to get in T's business and get her out of mine so I said, "T, what's up with Ricky? So you be giving it up on a regular basis now?"

T smiled and said with a sarcastic voice; "T and Ricky's business is their business."

Michelle sucked her teeth.

Before T opened her mouth, Lisa interrupted, "Let it go ladies, and just let it go."

The alcohol really began to take its affect and the weed was enlightening my thoughts. Smoked filled the air while Mary J Blige's "My Life" CD played.

"Sasha, you always listening to this shit. When you gonna let it go, play some Erykah Badu or something upbeat. Not this I'm going down." T rambled on, "always listening to old shit."

Now I knew it. We were drunk because T began barking like a pit bitch, Lisa began groping her throat and fiddling in her hair. Michelle was quiet as if she wasn't even with us. I began talking shit about anything that came to mind. "Yo why is it that men can't handle being with one woman? If we started that shit, we would be whores, oops, too late!"

We all started laughing.

"I mean I understand if it is a hit and go relationship, like me and Damon was, we had an understanding. But men still feel the need to be about other women, like that shit just comes naturally."

"I know, girl" T stormed in, "Linc doesn't understand that I have wings and I have to fly out of the coop. He just wouldn't understand. That is why I have to keep things from him."

"So you're saying Linc can't handle it, but you couldn't handle it when Ricky was messing around either."

"It's just like you to throw shit in my face...."

I interrupted. "All I'm saying..."

"You say too much, Sash, just keep your critical opinion to yourself. Yes, I knew about Ricky's flings, but I could handle it. It didn't matter cause he was bringing it all home to me. Them bitches just got dick. Ricky really loved me. I just over did it by the whole marriage thing. I shouldn't have pushed for it."

"Hold up," Lisa interrupted. "Are you saying it was cool for Ricky to leave you standing at the alter because you pushed him into the marriage?"

"No Lisa, I'm saying I understand why he did what he did. I pushed him into another woman's arms. The way our relationship worked was, I knew where we stood with each other at all times. I was happy with him and if he fooled around with some other chick, it was all good, as long as I didn't find out about it. Somewhere down the road the rules changed, I wanted him for myself, and I thought marriage would do that, so I let influences about the brass ring get into my head and into my relationship. But the truth was I was happy how things were. You see, Lisa, men are going to be men no matter what. Good or bad, dogs, players whatever. They get away with what you let them. Our relationship was no questions asked. The moment I tried to change that, he made the decision to leave or stay. He left. Don't get me wrong, Lisa, I was hurt a lot from that, and I have learned a lot, but I am not mad at him any more. I know to you guys it may seem like I hate men, I don't. Linc lets me get away with whatever he desires. I am not happy with Linc, I never will be, because he isn't Ricky and that is what I am used to. He is my passion, my soul mate."

My headspun. "T, you're losing me. A minute ago you couldn't stand men, let alone Ricky. Now you're saying he's your soul mate, what the hell is that about? You beat my head in about Montel, but then you forgive Ricky, like that shit never happened. You sound like you want to get back with him. I think you've had too much to drink."

"See Sash, that's why on some topics, especially men, we have to be silent or fake the front, because none of us understands what the other one is going through. No matter how much we whine about our problems, we run right back to them. So what does it matter. I know what I'm saying, Sash. Just like no one can tell you shit about Montel, or Michelle about Jamal, and we all told you, Lisa, not to marry that fool Jake. We don't listen."

"So what you saying? We aren't true friends, we are faking with each other." I questioned.

"No, Sasha, I am saying, it's your life. Only you can decide how to live it. Choices you make are your choices, no matter what influences brought you to that decision in your life. If push comes to shove, we are true friends, because no matter what nigga has done us wrong we stick together like family and that is how it should be. Yes we judge each other, but we only do that from our view. That's something that can't be helped."

"I understand what you're saying, T, and I agree. You still need to mind you business about Montel and I." I smiled.

"You crazy, girl."

Lisa bursted out, "Oh I think I need a hug."

"You stupid too, Lisa," T bursted out.

Michelle had been silent the whole time. It took me six wine glasses and three blunts to realize that Michelle had not even smoked or had that many wine sips, her glass was still half full. I began, "Michelle, what's up? You aren't drinking tonight?"

Michelle held on to her cup, as if she didn't want anyone to notice she hadn't been drinking.

"What is wrong, Chelle?" Lisa said.

Michelle began to open her mouth stuttering words out, "Well, I, see, I was going to tell you guys, but, well anyways, the reason I'm not partaking in the intoxication process is because I am pregnant."

A dead silence filled the room. No congratulations or nothing, just silent mouths. The CD began to skip; Lisa got up quickly to stop it. T cleared her throat.

I had to be the one to begin this episode. "How far along are you?"

"Just a couple of weeks, I found out last week."

A long pause fell through for the next question. "Well are you keeping it?" Lisa asked.

"Of course," Michelle said with certainty.

T interrupted, trying to hold back intoxicated words, "I will say it again, influences or not, we make our own choices, and Michelle you have just made the biggest mistake. How long are you going to let Jamal get his way? He continues to knock you up, and you play house and then he dips out on you for questionable reasons."

I interrupted, "T, it is her life, you just said…"

"I know what I said, Sash, I just hate to see you like this, Michelle."

"At least I'm not fucking someone else's husband. Shit, if you were to get pregnant, it would be a bastard child. Oops, then again, you probably wouldn't know who the father was."

T dashed at her with a fist. Michelle fell back. I grabbed T's arm and Lisa grabbed the other. We tried our hardest to hold her down.

Michelle stood up and starting ranting, "Look at you, T, ready to swing at me, for what? I am telling the truth that you can't handle. Yes we make choices and your choices definitely aren't any better than mine. How dare you judge me?"

T kept silent trying to hold back angry words.

"The truth is T, you are a hypocrite. You can't stand that I'm on my third child and you have nothing but empty arms."

Even that blow was too low for friendship; I let T's arm go. Lisa tried to hold T back, but she couldn't. T darted up and pushed Michelle to the floor. They tussled and tussled. Lisa tried hard to break them up. After a few smacks and kicks, I helped Lisa hold T back.

Michelle stood up, "None of you are my true friends. All you do is judge me and tell me how fucked up my life is, but when the topic hits your way, your lips get tight. Fuck you all." She ran out and slammed her door.

The events that happened went too fast for me to grasp. We were drunk, and it was time for us to go to bed. None of us said anything. We went to bed with the hopes that this would blow over the next morning.

CHAPTER ELEVEN

I dropped Lisa and her daughter, Jasmine, off first. Lisa said she had to be home in time to straighten up, D was coming over tonight. She spoke softly and quietly to him on her cell phone on the way from the Cape. T was silent. Michelle rode in the back with her two boys. She had not said a word to T or Lisa. The most she said to me was "What time are we leaving?" I knew this was going to be a long ride home. The ladies had argued before and gotten into physical fights, but this seemed different.

After I dropped everyone off, I checked my messages. To my surprise, there was nothing from Montel, no cell or phone messages. A familiar voice clogged my voicemail though, "Sash, we need to talk. Sash, you were supposed to handle this. Sash, you are really playing with fire and I don't want to be the bad guy in this, but you have to do what we discussed."

Seven damn messages from that Detective Perry. Was he straight stalking me? I told him I would speak to Raymond when he got back. It wasn't my fault Raymond had stayed in New York for what seemed like a month. Besides he didn't start work until next month and he and Tasha needed this time alone, they were about to have a baby. Anyways, I don't know what Michael was sweating, Ray didn't do anything. Tina just wanted him back, and she needed to give it up. I thought this would blow over, but I guess not.

I had been paging Montel for like an hour. He was supposed to meet me at the rental place at 2 p.m. so I could drop off this truck and go home. I missed him and I wanted to spend some quality time, damn it. *Where the hell is he?*

I waited until about 3, and then caught a cab home. By now I was seriously pissed. Not only had Montel not returned my pages, but he also left me high and dry at the car rental place. *If he doesn't have his ass at my house when I get home it will be on.* Insecure thoughts didn't fill my head. Anger was all I was burning off of. Montel knew that shit wasn't right, how was he going to just leave me stranded?

As the cab pulled up to my house, I gave the driver a twenty. He didn't even ask if I wanted change, bastard, men were just bastards! They take women for all they got, and we just let them, hoping the love is still there. Fuck that. The way I was feeling, Montel could drop all my keys to the house and cars in my mailbox, cause this shit was about to be over.

As I walked up the stairs, Raymond and Tasha were on their way out. I was so concerned about Montel that I forgot to tell him about Tina. I figured we would talk later. As I shuffled through my bag to look for my keys, the door opened.

"Where you been?" Montel had the audacity to ask.

I stood in the doorway with my head tilted and a look of confusion on my face. My words went out of control. "Where the fuck were you? I been at that damn rental place for an hour waiting on you and my fucking car, and you have the balls to ask me where have I been?"

Montel put his hands up in a motion to stop, but I kept going. With my arms waving high, I said, "Hello, earth to Montel, where the fuck were you? Don't even think you are going to tell me you didn't get my pages, because your pager is right here." I picked it up, "Here right here, now what, and what do you have to say for yourself?"

Before Montel could open his mouth, I continued, "You're tired, you're tired and you're trifling. How are you going to leave me high and dry? No concern for me at all. You disgust me. Get out of my way. Get out of my house. Give me my keys. Scram. Run along now, doggy…"

I went on and on as I threw my bag on the sofa and slouched in the chair. Montel slammed the door, threw the keys I gave to him and began to gather his things, not saying a word. I stared at this man like he was crazy. I know he wasn't pissed with me.

As he finished gathering his things and made his way out the door, I said, "You don't have anything to say for yourself?"

Without a word he came close to me as if he wanted to kiss me. He leaned in and with one hand braced himself on the sofa and with the other hand pushed the button to the answering machine on the table behind the sofa. The seven messages that Michael left me played. Without a word, Montel left and closed the door behind him.

I stood there in shock. I know he can't think there's anything going on with Michael and me. True, he left plenty of messages, but they were about Ray, not me and not him. How could he get that confused? He was jealous. He thought I had something else going on the side. I didn't, but to think he was just as insecure about me as I was about him. Wow, maybe we weren't from different planets.

I knew I could straighten this out with him, if I talked to him. I would just leave him a sweet message and that would be that. I dialed his pager and waited for the prompt to leave a message. "Hey baby, its me, I'm really sorry about going off on you today, I was real pissed with you because I thought, well it doesn't matter, I was wrong. And about Michael, he's a detective working on a case with Raymond; that is it. There is no he and I, if you don't believe me, come down to the station with Raymond and me when he makes his statement. This was all a big misunderstanding and I don't want to lose you over something silly like this. Call me, I love you, bye." *That should do it, Montel will be back by the early morning*, I thought.

As I relaxed and unwound in my empty home, I took a bath and fantasized about all the things I was going to do to Montel when he came home. I would tie him up and put a blindfold over his eyes. Then I would strip him and cover him with heated baby oil. After that, I would place each of my breasts against his mouth, one by one. I would sit on his penis with just my thongs on and lick his body from head to toe. Then I would get up and leave him there for a couple of minutes until he started moaning and begging for me to come back. Oooh weeee, the thought gave me chills up my spine.

After nine o'clock hit, I read a book. As eleven o'clock hit, I got my clothes ready for work. When one in the morning hit, I realized no one was calling, especially not Montel. Did he get my message? Was he still angry? I wished I knew the answer. The fact was, he had not called and my night of possibilities was over. I hoped Montel and I weren't. Great, this was a perfect day. Michelle isn't talking to the ladies, Michael is on my back, Raymond is probably in jail because I didn't tell him about Tina, and Montel is pissed at me over some bullshit. I shut off my light and pulled the covers up, thanking the Lord for this day and asking for another chance tomorrow.

By the end of the week with no Montel, I found myself in a stupor. I was a love-sick fool who felt her chance at happiness had slipped through her fingers. This was all just a misunderstanding. If I could only speak to him, this could be straightened out. I was a mess.

I tried to speak to Lisa about it, but she was off somewhere with D. I called T; she was chasing Ricky and dodging Linc. As for Michelle, she needed time to cool off, and realize we were still her girls. I was all alone.

Work consumed me, and it was the only thing keeping me afloat. In the past week, I have worked fifty-five hours at the hospital and the clinic for women's health. I delivered like sixteen babies, performed twenty-eight pap smears and counseled a dozen women, mostly young, on safe sex and breast cancer. Coming home to an empty house wasn't something I looked forward to every night, so I slept in the hospital most of the time. I had my calls forwarded and still no Montel. I mean damn, how long you can stay mad at someone, and for nothing!

Montel, of course, was blowing this out of proportion. The question was why? My imagination began to take over. Where was he? Who was he with? If this was what I was like without him for a week, imagine forever. I needed some help.

I finally made it home one evening; the smell of his cologne had finally left, his things were gone. I couldn't bear to look at the picture we took while we were in L.A. Was he just busy? Did he get my message? What was I going to do if this was it? If I wasn't so perplexed about his absence, I think I would have cried every night. After watching a dozen movies, I began to search for my phone book and realized I had thrown it away. I knew Damon's number by heart, but I couldn't bear to call. I was lonely, a place I hadn't been in a long time.

Sure, I didn't have fulfilling love-blown relationships in the past, but I had some sort of outlet. I had the girls, I had the flings, the regulars, I had it all. I traded it all in for Montel, a man whom I loved for so long. I believed in sacrifices, and I believed that he was worth it. My life seemed better when I was with him. I had fallen into the "you need a man in your life to have a life syndrome" and I didn't know how to pull myself out.

After two weeks, I realized Montel wasn't going to call. I guessed it was over, time for me to move on. After countless attempts for Detective Perry to catch up with Raymond, I finally arranged a meeting between the two. We agreed that he didn't have to come down to the station. Michael was pulling all the strings. I got up early to fix up the place. I made brunch, and got dressed, just going through the motions, not even realizing that my appearance wasn't the same. I didn't feel like me, I felt really vulnerable and sensitive.

Raymond came downstairs and offered to help, but I was finished. "How long is this going to take? I have a game with the little ones and Tasha has an appointment with that doctor you referred her too."

I stepped back and looked at my brother in a whole new light. He had grown up so fast, he was taking on all his responsibilities, and living up to the man I knew he could be. I felt so proud, like I was the mommy. At least one of us was going to be happy. He felt strongly about his relationship with Tasha and planned on marrying her, starting a family the right way. "Ray Ray, I haven't been around you much lately, but you sure have changed. Besides this little incident, you haven't brought any drama to my house yet. You really are becoming a man. I can't call you Ray Ray any more. It's Raymond, right?"

Raymond giggled and put his arm around me, "Yeah, I know, I am the shit!"

We laughed.

"Are you all right, Sash? You aren't going to start getting emotional are you?"

"No, Raymond, I'm just in awe of you right now. One minute you are little Ray, and the next you are about to be a dad."

"I know, Sash, don't worry though. I'm going to make sure my son has his shit together. I'm going to teach him about being a man, a better man than me. I am going to show him the world is at his feet, he just has to learn how to play the game. Raymond's face just lit up talking about his future son.

"Hey Ray, how you know it is going to be a boy, what if it's a girl?" Close space

"I want her to be just like you."

I almost cried.

"Ay you, don't get all girly on me now."

"I am just in a weird place right now, and I don't feel like myself."

"Yeah, that nigga got you bugging. Stop playing yourself, Sasha; you know what needs to be done. Cut him lose."

"I know, but it's hard when you have your mind set on something, and it doesn't turn out the way you hoped after you put all your energy and all your emotion into it."

"I know what you're saying, Sash, but just like basketball, if you don't win, you either play again or take up a new sport."

"Whatever, I just have to figure this one out on my own."

"Yo, what time is this guy going to get here? I have things to do."

"He said two, and its two now, so it shouldn't be long."

"He needs to hurry up."

"Do you have your story straight, you know what you're going to tell him?"

"Yeah, I saw Tina that night, we talked, I told her it was over, she flipped, started hitting me, I pushed her, and she started crying, yelling names…"

"Wait a minute, Ray, you pushed her?"

"Yeah, to get her off of me. Not in a violent way, but in a get off me way."

"How hard did she fall?"

"I don't know. Once I pushed her, I walked out of there; she was yelling shit as I was leaving."

"Damn, you pushed her! She could use that if she wanted to."

"Yeah, I know but I'm telling you, if we get the lawyers involved, she'll back off."

"I hope so."

The doorbell rang; it was Michael. We went over what needed to be said. He told us he would let us know and Raymond needed to get in touch with a lawyer just in case she wanted to take this thing further. Raymond thanked Michael for coming.

We held onto a couple of laughs as we drank and ate.

The conversation, I noticed, was turning into men against women, so I had to defend myself. Michael started it, "Some sisters today are so trifling, and I just don't want to be bothered."

Raymond gave him dap.

"Excuse me, brothers are trifling as well. It depends on who you're messing with."

"Whatever, you women think us men speak a different language than you. But the truth is we have feelings like you and don't want to get hurt like you, so we hide from who you want us to be."

“Well, you need to stop hiding, so we all can get together and have a good time, you know. The way I feel right now is all men can kiss my ass.”

Michael said quickly, “Hey don’t they already do that?”

Ray and Michael laughed.

“If you must know, Detective, I too get done wrong; I am not always the bad girl, as you would like to believe.”

Michael smiled, “I understand you, more than you think. But you, just like every other woman looking for love, are searching in the wrong place. Your ideal man is just that, an ideal. Stop loving with your mind, and start loving with your heart.”

“Where did that come from?”

“I tend to get deep about these things. I was divorced about seven years ago. I married my high school sweetheart because of what I thought she was instead of what I felt about her. So that ended, and now I know what’s what. And on that note, if you will excuse me, I must use your bathroom please.”

“You know where it is.”

As Michael got up, Raymond looked at me in a weird way.

“What’s going on here?” he asked.

“Nothing,” I said innocently.

“Yeah whatever, I am out. You two love birds are going to have to do without me.”

“We aren’t any lovebirds!”

“Whatever!”

Raymond left. Michael came back with a look of surprise. We were alone. To an even bigger surprise, we didn't say a word, no insults, and no sarcasm. We just sat there.

"I better get going," he said.

"I'm sure duty calls or something. Hey, thanks a lot for what you did today. I guess I figured you wrong, you're not such a bad guy, decent even."

"I guess, I come down hard on you sometimes." Michael admitted.

"Sometimes, try all the time, with the exception of today."

"True, I don't know, you just spark something in me that I can't control."

I was confused.

"I mean, never mind. I'll talk to you later."

As he opened the door, I reached for his arm to tell him to stay, maybe there was more here than just two people trying their best not to get along. I don't know what I was feeling, lonely, desperate, but I wanted him to stay. Before I could get the words out of my mouth, the door opened, and to an even bigger surprise, Montel was in my doorway.

CHAPTER TWELVE

"Yeah right Ms. Sasha," Montel said in disgust as he rolled his chinky eyes at me and walked away.

Of course I dashed after him. "Wait, Montel it's not what you think." I grabbed his arm; he snatched it away. "Would you just listen to me? What did you come by for?"

Montel turned around and said to me with a look of craziness in his eyes, "What did I come by for?"

Before I could explain, Michael came onto the scene, like he was coming to my rescue. The same damn manner he used when the cops had Ray handcuffed on my porch. Michael said, "Excuse me, I'm Detective Perry." Michael extended his hand for Montel to shake, but Montel looked at his hand like, *whatever*. "I don't know what you thought, but I'm here working on a case for Raymond, Sash's brother." (As if Montel didn't know who Raymond was.) We're through here, Sasha; I'll be in touch with Raymond and you when I hear from the D.A.'s office. Take care, oh and nice to meet you, Montel."

Michael walked away, but gave me a disapproving look and kept going. It was one of those looks like he was disgusted with how I behaved, and couldn't believe I was chasing this man. Well, whatever Michael thought, it didn't matter, Montel was here and I just knew he wanted to work things out.

"Montel, it's not what you think, I know it seems like Detective Perry is always around and that's because there is always drama. I told you about the dude who wrecked my place and I also told you about the charges being brought up on Ray, so I don't understand where this attitude is coming from. Talk to me, I know you didn't come all the way over here to pout."

"No, Sasha, I didn't come over here to pout. I came to see you and I missed you. It seems every time I come around, or I am not around, that cop cat is. You say there's nothing going on with him, but he acts like there is."

"What are you talking about?"

"Sash, I know men, and that man is into you, so I don't want him around you if Ray isn't present."

"Montel you're being barbaric, you can't forbid me to see anyone!"

"I'm not forbidding you; I'm just telling you I don't like it. And if you cared about me at all, you would understand!"

"I do care about you baby, I love you. When you were gone I thought it was over, you didn't call. You didn't return my messages."

"I needed some time to think, that shit that went down with us was crazy, and I felt crazy, out of control, I didn't realize how deep my feelings ran for you. But, I can't stand the thought of you with some other man, and I don't know what I would do if you were."

I put my arms around Montel's waist and buried my face into his chest. "You won't have to worry about that; I only love you."

Montel pressed his head on the top of mine. "I am glad to hear it, because you are my world."

We just stood there, in each other's arms, like time would stop for us. Montel really loved me; he just needed time. I kept saying that in my head over and over again, so it would stick, I would believe in it. Chasing away all doubts, chasing away all fears. He loved me.

The next couple of months got crazier. I saw less of Montel; I thought we were supposed to be growing. The baby boom hit like the summer heat. I delivered more newborns than I think I ever had in my one year of being an obstetrician. They were dropping like flies. I was busy delivering babies, and Montel was trying to get this new group off the ground, so he was traveling more.

Lisa, Tamieka, Tasha, and Ray were throwing me this surprise birthday party they didn't think I knew about. So I was real excited about that!

Michelle still was keeping herself distant from the ladies. I called her, but she didn't return my calls. I dropped off little gifts for the boys, but she wasn't around. I really needed to know what was going on with her. How was the baby doing? What hospital, what doctor? I needed to know. I had to make sure she was all right. We always stuck together, and the way she was shutting out the ladies couldn't be healthy for her or the baby. That's why I was going to make it a point to see how she was doing.

At the end of the day, I had called in a number of favors to find out who Michelle's obstetrician was. I finally got the necessary info. Coincidently, Michelle's doctor worked out of the same hospital I did. Her name was Dr. Matilda Roebeck. She was one of my instructors in Medical school, a real bitch! She and I didn't see eye to eye, and were always getting into debates about right and wrong. That was the past though; I hoped she would have calmed down by now. She was such a stickler for the rules.

On my way home, I stopped by Dr. Roebeck's office. Matilida the Hun wasn't there, but her secretary was. Her secretary happened to be Tamela Johnson, a friend of my cousin Tanya. So of course, I used this edge. "Hey girl, whazzup, how you been?"

Tammy rose to hug me. "Oh, I'm fine, are you a doctor yet?"

"Yeah girl, I finished my residency last year."

"Oh that is so wonderful, do you need a secretary?"

"Tammy you crazy, don't you work for what's her name?"

Tammy gave me this look and said, "Exactly! I can't stand that heifer."

This was even better.

"Have you spoken to Tanya, Sash?"

"No, I haven't but I plan to soon."

"Yeah, we kind of lost touch when she got married but we will hook up soon."

"Hey Tammy, could you do me a favor? I need to look at my friend's file, you remember Michelle?"

"Oh yeah, I seen her in here, she's having another baby?"

"Yeah, I know, I just want to see how she is doing, we haven't spoken in a minute, but I'm worried about her."

"Say no more, Dr Roebeck is going to be out of the office for at least another hour, she's delivering, so help yourself."

"Thanks Tammy, I'm going to be just a minute."

"That's fine; I'm going to get a soda anyway."

"All right. If I don't see you, take care."

"You too, Sasha."

I looked in the E section of Dr. Roebuck's files and came across Edwards, Michelle. I looked through the folder; everything seemed to be in order. *Damn. Michelle's almost six months pregnant, she didn't look that big that weekend. What are these other tests? Michelle needs to take better care of herself, I don't care what's going on, I'm going over there today to let her know the deal.* You'd think she was highly experienced in this and would now what she's doing. Then again, like I said earlier, the ladies need the ladies.

Just when I was about to put the file down, I noticed another slip of paper that read CONFIDENTIAL. It was an HIV test and to my horror, it read positive. I thought I was going to collapse or cry. I quickly tucked that slip back in the file, dashed out, closed the door and just made it out when; Dr. Roebeck came into the office.

"Freeman, what are you doing in my office?"

I quickly said, "I was coming to see you."

"Did you not notice I was not here? Why are you coming out of my office?"

"I didn't see anyone, so I figured you were in your office, so I checked and you weren't there, and here you are."

"Is there something you want to tell me, Dr. Freeman?"

I shrugged. "No."

"Then why are you here?"

"Oh yeah, that's right, I was looking for some advice about a patient."

"Advice, you have never come to me about advice, so why come now?"

"You know you're right, Dr. Roebeck, I never have, and now I know why, you ask too many questions and I never get an answer, so what's the point, I mean really!"

I gave her the same look I gave her when she was my instructor. *Bitch!* She looked at me funny, as though she knew I was up to something. I stared her down, and kept going out of the door, out of her office, and I prayed that I made it out of the woods with her.

I didn't know how I was feeling, on my way to Michelle's house. Not only did I violate her right to privacy and put my job on the line, I failed her as a friend. We all did, who knew what she was going through, right now. I began to cry. I thought about all the fun we had as kids, and then I thought about her kids, and then I thought about her unborn child, and then I thought about Jamal. That low down, dirtball, bastard. How could he do this! If I felt this way, I could only imagine how Michelle was feeling.

I reached her house door; I tried to get what I was going to say to her straight as I rang the doorbell. She answered the door with a surprised look on her face. I just hugged her tight. "Michelle, I missed you so much, don't go!"

Michelle began, "Sasha what the hell is wrong with you?"

I wiped my tear before she could see it, "Nothing, I am just all emotional, my period is coming."

"Don't be talking about periods around here; I won't see one for a long time."

I laughed. "So how have you been? I call you but you don't call me back, whazzup with that?"

"I just needed time to think."

"I know, Michelle, you don't owe me or anyone else an excuse, and I just missed you that's all. We all missed you."

"I missed you guys too. So what you been up to?"

"Montel and I are still kickin it. Ray's girl, Tasha, is twenty-four weeks pregnant. I haven't heard anything about that crazy Tina girl; hopefully she dropped the charges. And the ladies are planning me a surprise party that I am not suppose to know about."

"I see. How are the ladies?"

Just then my cell phone rang. "Hello"

"Sash, it's me, Linc done found out about Ricky and shit is just a mess, where are you?"

"Michelle's. Why don't you come through?"

Michelle heard T, through the phone and grabbed it from me, "Yeah why don't you bring your stank ass over here," Michelle said in a playful way.

T hung up, I called Lisa up for reinforcements, and the ladies were back on! The four of us stood outside on Michelle's porch, getting everything out. Michelle apologized to T for saying what she did, and T apologized to Michelle for hitting her.

T admitted she really felt bad, "If anything were to happen to your baby, I would just kill myself."

"Okay, so this one will be your godchild then, how about that?" Michelle said.

The thought left T speechless; they just hugged each other.

I had my own thoughts going through my head, like *one day T will have to take that baby in.* I tried not to be sad, I couldn't let on that I knew. I kept the happy front going. "So T, what up with Linc, he mad?"

"Of course he's mad, but more so hurt!"

"You mean to tell me you care about Linc's feelings?" I said, playfully.

"Yes, I do, but I don't want to be with him, I want to be with Ricky."

"Oh no, here we go again," Michelle said.

Lisa said, "Well you've had them both for months, now you have to choose. You know what kind of men they both are. The question is, who are you going to be happy with? Are you going to be happy with Linc, a man who loves you unconditionally? Or are you going to be happy with Ricky, a man who is obligated to another woman?"

T said, "Well, that isn't a hard choice, Ricky is the man for me. He and I fit together. Linc and I don't make sense; he needs someone, well like you Michelle, soft, motherly, home-body type, angelic. I'm rough around the edges and I like it rough around the edges. I need that drama in my life."

I questioned, "So what are you going to do?"

"I'm going to tell Linc the truth and take it from there."

"Well, all the power to you," I patted T on the back.

We all stood out there, talking for a while. My advice on the situation would be to let Ricky go, but you can't advise a woman in love, no one can. You have to figure it out for yourself. We understood each other. We tried so hard to be the better person or to head the better advice, but how could we, when we always ended up doing the opposite of what we should do? I just stood back and took a good look at my friends. I loved them no matter what; I accepted them no matter what. We all knew each other's business, even the most private, from the dirtiest to the cleanest. There was no need to front with them, for they knew who I truly was and would accept that no matter what. I would do the same for any of them, too.

I was so exhausted that day. I came home to an empty house. Montel still wasn't back from his trip. I checked my answering machine. No new messages. Oh well, I was getting used to the space that Montel and I come into. There were many nights I wished he were there with me, but what was the use, I didn't get any. I was becoming use to that too. I hadn't hit a dry spell in a very long, long time. I guess it did my mind some good; I began to see what was really important, and sex wasn't everything in a relationship. If I kept telling myself that, it would sink in like everything Montel said and did to me has.

I reached the top of my stairs and opened my bedroom door. To my surprise nothing but dim candle lights flickered in my room and rose petals covered my bed. As I stepped in, the door closed behind me, one hand from behind grabbed my waist the other hand brushed my cheek with a single rose. I turned around and saw Montel. He was dressed in nothing and ready to press on my soft body.

He placed his hand against my lips as I said, "I thought." He kissed me, and led me to the bathroom where he undressed me and gave me a bath. As he turned the radio on, he dried my body, lifted me to his waist and we fell on the rose- covered bed. His naked body pressed against my damp skin. He kissed my lips, my chin, and my neck. He gently grabbed my breasts and placed them in his mouth one by one, sucking them and biting them like watermelons. He continued licking me up and down as he turned me onto my stomach and licked down my spine. Jagged Edge's "I Just Got To Be" played on the radio.

Montel took a petal and swept it across my spot, he began to lick, and lick and lick. I was about to explode! He stopped, stared me dead in the face and said, "Do you like that?" in the sexiest, most sensual voice I have ever heard! I just nodded; I couldn't even speak.

I rose to my knees to meet him at the edge of the bed. He rose to his knees; he's still a little taller than me on his knees. I began to kiss him everywhere. I wrestled him down to the bed.

I crept up to him slowly as I went for his place. He moaned. I moaned.

I came up and sat on top of him as I licked his navel. He grabbed my hair; the tips of his fingers touched my roots. I licked his nipples then sucked on his neck. I reached his lips and he said to me, "I love you, Sasha."

I gave him a sexy smile as he rolled me over to be on top. Still grabbing my hair, he entered me; my legs were past my ears. He thrust slowly, I moaned every time. I rolled him over and rode him first frontward then backwards. His hands grabbed my breast; I could feel the explosion coming. I yelled out a load moan as I reached ecstasy.

Sitting on his lap, tears were coming out of my eyes, we both moved in the same motion as my legs were locked around his waist and my hands held his back in a bear hug. His face was buried in my neck. He moaned, and moaned and moaned. He reached his point and then lay back with me on top of him in our newborn suits. I kissed him and said, "I love you Montel."

We fell asleep in each other's arms, with not a care in the world.

CHAPTER THIRTEEN

I was on cloud nine at work the next morning. I was on cloud nine at the end of the workweek as well. Montel and I finally made love. He was worth waiting for. It was so beautiful I wanted to cry. I just knew everything would be uphill from now on. By the end of the workweek, I was even more excited because, come this time next week, I was on vacation for two weeks. If this wasn't heaven, I didn't know what was. Montel claimed he was taking me to L.A. again since we had such a good time there before. I couldn't wait.

I made my rounds, the new mothers were doing fine. No deliveries, surprisingly, and just two more hours left until freedom. I was going to use all the time I had to spend with my Montel. Since we made love, we could do it all the time. I couldn't wait to do the do.

My surprise birthday party was tomorrow night. I had a lot of things to do today so four o'clock needed to hit like right now. I began to make out my to-do list in my office. Hmm let's see, I need a new outfit for tomorrow, some shoes, some new earrings, some lingerie, some bath oils, some whipped cream, some cherries. Oops, my list was turning into a sexing list! I couldn't help it, I was so happy. My phone rang, *ooh, who is it, don't they know I am trying to get out of here like now?* I answered the phone, "Yes."

"Hello, Freeman, this is Dr. Roebeck, I know you were in my files last week, I am taking this up with the hospital board."

I cleared my throat, “Excuse me; I don’t know what you are talking about.”

“My secretary told me. You have a lot of explaining to do. I am setting up a meeting with the board today.” She hung up.

What the hell is going on around here? I know Tammy wouldn’t tell that gobbler anything! I rushed out of my office and down to hers. Dr. Roebeck wasn’t there, but Tammy was.

“Hey girl, whazzup!” Tammy said.

“What’s up,” I said in amazement. “What is up is that you told Dr. Frankenstein I was in her office. Duh!”

“Oh, well she figured it out for herself; I just reinforced it. No big deal.”

“No big deal! I could loose my license.”

“For what?”

“Haven’t you ever heard of patient confidentiality?”

“What? Michelle is your friend. By the way how is she doing?”

“Tammy, you are not with it, don’t you know anything about patient rights? Michelle is not my patient; therefore, I can’t look into her chart. Now if she happened to tell me something as a friend, then that is fine.”

“Oh I see, well I am sure it will work itself out. How is her hubby, Jamal, doing?”

“Why are you so interested in Michelle, you guys only met once when we were kids, you don’t even know Jamal?”

Just then a conversation came to mind, Tammy, the blackmailer. “Wait a minute, Tammy; I know you are not the Tammy who’s having an affair with Michelle’s husband?”

"Damn! Jamal told her? He is so stupid!"

I was amazed. This girl, my cousin's friend, had no clue! "Tammy you are fucking someone else's husband. You are fucking his family. Don't you even give a damn?"

"Frankly, I don't. That's on him. If the home was happy…"

"Don't give me that if the home was happy shit, if you were happy with yourself, you wouldn't be... Oh never mind, it's pointless, you are nasty and you better watch yourself."

"What is that supposed to mean?"

"It means Jamal has…" I stopped myself.

"Jamal has what a family?"

"Yes he has a family and you are not a part of it."

"Whatever, Sasha, you just don't understand the circumstances around it."

"I don't want to know. But I will tell you one thing, you keep your mouth shut about me being in this office and I won't tell Michelle where you work. She would choke you if she knew. And to think you can just sit there and sign her in for her doctor visits, while in the back of your mind you reminisce about sucking her husband's dick! You are sick Tammy, just trifling."

"Whatever, you just keep your end of the bargain."

I slammed the office door. Not only was I keeping a secret about Michelle's test, but now I would have to be quiet about this Tammy shit too. I just wanted to see if Michelle was okay. Damn it, I am too nosy!

I walked back to my office, and to my surprise, the chief of staff was waiting for me. Before he said a word, I tried to explain, "Look, Dr. Cooper, I can explain."

"No need, Dr. Freeman, you will have your say at the boards. For now it is best for you to take an extended vacation until this matter is cleared up."

My heart dropped, "Excuse me, am I being fired?"

"No, but this matter needs to be cleared up. Until then, I think it would be best that you…"

"That I what, leave the premises immediately? You haven't even heard my side of the story, and you are ready to throw me out of here."

"Dr. Freeman, I already told you, no one is throwing you out."

"Whatever, you are taking sides. Dr. Roebuck has hated me since med school and now she's trying to ruin me! I can't believe this. You're taking sides. Her case is bull."

"You will have your chance to defend yourself at the boards."

"Defend myself. I shouldn't have to! Whatever, I am out of here!"

I didn't even pack up my things, cause I knew I would be back! I am not going to let some two-bit old hag tell me what I can and cannot do. Talk about patient confidentiality! She had her patient's husband's mistress signing Michelle in, taking down all her information. This fucking hospital hasn't heard the last of me! I dashed out of there. Well, I got my vacation I always wanted. Who knew when I would work again? I was glad I saved up or else I would be in a shit load of trouble. The thought of Montel soothed me. I had to call him, and he knew how to comfort me. I got to my house to find a frail Tasha on my doorstep. "What's wrong, Tasha, where's Raymond?"

"They took him."

"Who took him?"

"I don't know," tears started pouring down her face; her speech got muffled.

"What's going on?"

"The police. Tina didn't drop the charges. That Detective called and tried to warn us, tried to have Ray's lawyer present. It just all happened so fast."

"Come on." I grabbed her arm and ran inside my house.

Michael left me several messages telling me to hurry down to the station before it gets too late and I won't be able to get Raymond out until Monday. That message was at 2 p.m., it was now 4:30 p.m. I called the station but Michael wasn't around.

I spoke to the desk clerk, who said, "No one is going to be bailed out tonight, and the judges will be gone by the time you get here."

I yelled at him, "We'll see about that!"

My thoughts raced. Who did I know who had connects. Tanya, she was a lawyer, she would know! I called her; it took several rings for her to answer. "Tanya," I said.

"Sash, is that you? What's up girlfriend, why haven't I heard from you?"

"There's no time for that. I need your help. Raymond's in jail, they're talking about no bail, and I want him out fucking tonight! You have to help me."

"Calm down Sash, I'll see what I can do. Meet me at the courthouse in twenty minutes."

I grabbed Tasha, who was still crying, by the arm, got in my car and sped off. By the time I got to the courthouse, it looked closed. Tanya met me there. We walked down the hall fast. She was dressed to the nines of course. She wore a skirt suit that fit her hourglass frame, white blouse, pumps, and hair pinned up. She had her glasses on, French manicured nails, and her makeup was flawless. My cousin Tanya didn't play! She walked down that hall with me as if she were running the place. Her light-skinned face kept turning back in forth, as she tried to explain the situation.

We stopped in front of the D.A.'s office. "All right, Sash, my field is entertainment law as you know. Luckily I know the D.A. She's a real bitch, but she likes it when I invite her to the celebrity parties, to feed her ego. Right now as it stands, Tina dropped the charges, but the D.A. wanted to take it further and is continuing this case in the name of the so-called people. Translation: she's running for some office and needs votes! The important thing today is to get Ray out. Since he's my cousin, that shouldn't be a problem. Your problem is going to be getting these charges dropped. I have no idea how that is going to play, but here's a card to a very good attorney second to Jonnie Cochran. He could have gotten Charlie Manson off! He's sweet on my mother, so he will take this case, but he normally doesn't deal with itty-bitty cases like this. He is very expensive, but that shouldn't be a problem since you are Ms. M.D., right?"

I quickly said, "Right." I didn't want to embarrass myself with what went on earlier, so I played along.

"Okay, Sash, here goes nothing. Oh and remember, let me do all the talking."

Tanya entered the room, "Devonia, how are you today, girl!" They hugged like they were old sorority sisters. "This is my cousin, Sasha Freeman."

"What kind of name is Sasha?"

I gave a look, but I kept my mouth shut, this wasn't about me.

"Alright, let's get down to business. Devonia, you have Raymond Freeman in custody. We want him out, what is it going to take?"

"Tanya, you get right down to business. It will take a signed confession and a plea of guilty."

I sucked my teeth. Devonia looked at me as if I offended her.

"Ha, ha, really, what is it going to take, D?"

"Given the aptitude of this case, I plan to take it all the way. Now, I can release him, but I'm starting right up with indictment charges, so you better move fast on this one. I can get the judge to set the bail for around five thousand."

I couldn't hold it in any longer. "Are you serious?"

"Ms. Freeman, I am very serious, your brother is going down and so is that Detective Perry. He handled this case all wrong. If I left it up to him, justice would never be served."

"Oh that is a bunch of bologna. Detective Perry is a good cop and the only place my brother is going is home to take care of his family, so you better back off sister!"

Tanya gave me that look of what the hell are you doing! "Will you excuse us?

Look Sasha, I told you I'm an entertainment lawyer, and although I may look like I belong on TV, I am not any entertainer and neither are you! So wait out here!"

I began to pace. Things were just spinning out of control. Tanya came out, "Ray will be released; his hearing is on Monday. Here is Martin's card, call him tonight. You almost blew it back there."

"I don't care. Raymond hasn't done a damn thing!"

"Look Sash, that is up to the judge to decide."

"Whatever, how much is bail?"

"I don't know, let's go down to the clerk's office and find out."

Raymond's bail was five thousand. His retainer would probably be more for this scum-ball lawyer, and my stash was about to dwindle away very quickly!

After we left the courthouse, Ray thanked Tanya for her help. So did I.

"Not a problem, but you can call a sister and let her know what is going on with y'all."

"I know, Tanya. I will definitely keep in touch."

I drove everyone back to the house. I wanted to scream! My day was hell. I called Montel. It took him three pages to call me back.

"What's wrong, Sasha? You sound upset."

"I just had a hell of a day, you know. Where are you?"

"I'm in Montreal with the group. I won't be back until late tonight. I'll call you tomorrow. Get some rest, sweetheart."

Great, my man couldn't comfort me. I couldn't go shopping, seeing how I didn't know where my next meal was coming from. I was in a tight squeeze! I ran my bath water, soaked for an hour, and went to bed. *Well tomorrow is my party. Yes, tomorrow will be a better day.*

I woke up feeling yesterday's heat. I decided to go shopping anyways; after all it was my birthday. I was twenty-eight. Wow, you can do a lot at twenty-eight. I picked up a nice outfit for the party with some matching shoes, got my hair, nails and toes done. I was ready for the evening. I didn't know who or how my friends intended to get me to this party, but as long as I got there I was happy. Lisa called me and told me we were going out tonight to some club and for me to be ready at nine o'clock. I said okay, as if I didn't know about this party! Ray and Tasha had already left. I wondered if Montel knew about this party. I hoped so, who would be my date? Anyway, T came to pick me up and off we went.

As I walked into this so-called club, the parking lot was full of BMWs, Lexes, Jeeps, and Benzes. I noticed they invited some high society folks. Oh, my party was about to be ignorant off the hook! I didn't see Montel's car out there though. I reached the door and everyone yelled surprise! I did the right thing. I pretended to be surprised! The party was jumping. Cousin Tanya and Aunt Mimi were there. T invited Ricky. Michelle and Jamal were there. A few buddies from work. Some friends from high school were there also. My college roommate, Marian, was there with her husband, David. Some of my parent's friends were there. It was off the hook. It is nice to know that you are loved. After the day before, I had I needed this real bad! I found Lisa in the bathroom.

"Hey girl, surprise," Lisa said.

"Thank you, girl! Is Montel here?" I asked.

"Ray told him about it and for him to be here. That fine-ass Detective is here though."

"Where? Tell me where, so I can avoid him."

"Why would you want to do that?"

"I'm just kidding. Actually, I need to talk to him about Ray. But if Montel is here, I don't want to be around him. Montel claims Michael wants me, but I don't think so. Just to keep the peace, I want to keep a distance, you know?"

"You really love him don't you?"

"Yeah I do, Lisa, I really do. Where is this D you are talking about, can we finally meet?"

"Yeah, he seemed to disappear after we yelled surprise!"

"Well go find him, girl, I have to meet the man who has put a smile on your face!"

We left the bathroom. I searched for Montel and tried to avoid Michael. I saw a familiar face through the crowd. No, it couldn't be. "Damon, what are you doing here? Who told you about my party? Oh that is really nice of you to come. How have you been?"

"Oh, I am fine. Look, honestly Sash, I didn't know believed me on that one!"

"What are you talking about Damon?"

Just then, Lisa came over, "Oh there you are, and I have been looking all over for you?"

"Well I'm right here," I said as I started to do the dip dance, I was starting to feel the alcohol.

"Not you silly. Sasha, I want you to meet D. D, this is Sasha."

My mouth dropped. "What? Damon is your D?"

"You two know each other?" Lisa looked confused.

Lisa, Damon, oh I mean D, and I stood there in shock!

CHAPTER FOURTEEN

As I stood there, words could not be thought out. This was too much of a shock. Did Damon plan this? Was this revenge? Lisa, did she know too? I never introduced them. They only knew him by Damon, not D. Still Damon has been to my house many nights, he had to have seen Lisa's picture. This couldn't have been any damn coincidence. Damon began to explain, but I had already made up my mind.

"Wait a minute, before everyone gets all bent! Lisa, I had no idea the Sasha you knew was the Sasha I know." Lisa sucked her teeth. Damon turned to me. "Now, Sasha, I had no idea Lisa was your girl!"

"Yeah right, How could you sit there and lie to my face! You mean to tell me you never once saw Lisa's picture in my house? You never once heard me mention her name? You didn't see Raymond here?"

Damon put his hands up. "I knew when I got here. When I saw your brother, when I saw your picture on the cake. I knew then. I never knew before."

Lisa cut in, "So why did you insist on me calling you D?"

"What! I like you to call me that." He batted his eyes. I had to admit that Damon was one of the smoothest brothers I knew. There he stood with his Armani suit on, clean cut, shaved, Rolex blinging on his wrist, manicured fingers with the shiniest of shoes. Damon had the smile that would draw a woman's attention. I got wet when he would start to flirt.

Damon had it going on. His maple-brown smooth skin and bubbled light-brown eyes made him the handsomest of men. I could see how Lisa was smitten with him. I was too. But I let him go.

"Look, I didn't know, Sash, and I didn't know, Lisa, baby. I can see this is awkward, so I will leave." He kissed Lisa on the lips, whispered something in her ear, he turned to me and said, "Happy birthday, Sasha." He left as Lisa turned her head from Damon's disappearing back; she rolled her eyes and looked dead at me.

"So that was your booty call, Damon? How could I be so naïve to think he only wanted me? Didn't you diss him? He was probably trying to get back at you."

I knew what Lisa was saying and I also knew what she really thought. On the forefront, she thought Damon was wrong but in the back of her mind, she hated me. She hated the fact that men were always about me. I know she felt second best when we went out, men were attracted to me first, then her. I knew she couldn't stand that so I always flocked them off to her. Lisa was my girl, a true friend, but I know them green eyes came out once in a while. I felt like screaming inside. I didn't know what Damon's motives were. Was he just as crazy as Jason? I couldn't get Lisa's face out of my head when she introduced us. She was so happy. Now her face was gloomy, hiding her true feelings of hurt. I couldn't deal with this. Where the hell was Montel?

"Lisa have you seen Montel."

"Nah," she said.

Just then, Michelle and T came over.

"Where did mystery man go?" T asked.

Quickly, Lisa said, "Ask Sasha."

I looked at her with a scold. Was she trying to blame this on me? "Whatever, did you guys invite Montel?"

T answered, "Raymond told him about it, he should be here. Maybe he's just late"

"Or maybe he's not coming," Lisa said.

I tried to ignore this girl but she was beginning to piss me off. "Yo Lisa, cool it!" I said.

"What's going on, Sash? What did you do?" Michelle questioned.

"What did I do?"

"Yeah, what happened to D?"

"D is Damon, Sasha's booty call!" Lisa said.

Mouths dropped; hands covered them.

"What!" T said. "Men are scandalous!"

Michelle asked, "Did he know you were friends, Sasha?"

"He claims he had no idea," Lisa answered.

"Well then, what is the issue?" Michelle questioned.

T couldn't help herself, "It's always like you, Michelle, to believe every word that comes out of a man's mouth."

"Fuck you T, don't go there with me. I don't see Linc on your arm, just that trifling Richard."

"Well, where is Jamal, trying to find his next victim?"

"All right, damn it!" I said in frustration. "This is supposed to be my birthday."

"Whatever!" Michelle grabbed Lisa by the arm as to console her.

T stood by my side with that same old attitude, "niggas ain't shit!" That was how we were, T and I were more alike and Michelle and Lisa were more alike. I guess cause they had kids and been married. That would explain their bond. Nonetheless, I was too aggravated to explain. I just wanted to know where the hell Montel was.

The night went on song after song, hour after hour. There was still no sign of Montel. We danced, we ate, and we drank. The girls each gave a speech about me, the me they knew. Raymond also spoke. I discussed Raymond's case with Aunt Mimi and Tanya. I cut the cake. I drank some more. Still no Montel. It was a quarter till 1 a.m. The last song played I had no one to dance with. I sat holding on to my bottle of Moet.

A tall figure walked through the crowd. It was none other than Detective. Perry. He reached his hand out for mine. I thought, *Why not?* Montel stood me up, he couldn't get mad if he wasn't here to see me dance with him. I stood up and let Michael lead me to the floor. We danced. I even buried my head in his shoulder as Jagged Edge's song played *I just got to be*, the same song Montel and I made love to. Where was he? Did Raymond give him the right information? I was vexed to why he didn't show up. Maybe he would surprise me at home. I lifted my head from Michael's shoulder and looked around. No sign of him.

"Face it, he isn't coming." Michael said.

I looked at Michael in the weirdest way. "How do you know?" I said.

"Look Sash, I don't know how to tell you this, but your so-called man is an asshole. Wait before you say anything. I care about you, Sasha Freeman, and I know I always give you a hard time, but I do. Take this from a friend, let him go." Michael lifted my chin when he said that, it was almost as if he wanted to kiss me. Instead he stared at me and said, "Do you know how beautiful you are?"

I broke away as he grabbed my arm. I wiped my tear; I didn't want him to see. "Just leave me alone Michael."

He grabbed me and held me in a bear hug.

"Listen Sasha, I am only telling you this as a friend. On my way here, I got a call to check out a party in a hotel that was making a lot of noise. Since I was in the area I checked it out. I knocked on the door to the hotel suite. A young brother opened the door. He was throwing a bachelor's party for his man. I asked if he could keep it down. Man to man I understood what this party meant to his man. I didn't want to kill the party, just keep it under control. He understood and was like 'Cool.' This was a wild party. There were drinks, drugs, everything, even strippers. Just as I was about to leave the strippers came out, as a man I wanted a peek. So I did just that. To my surprise, the strippers were advised to start with the groom, who sat in a chair, 6 foot 2, light-skinned with chinky eyes. The groom was Montel."

CHAPTER FIFTEEN

Michael stood there with me. I couldn't move for a second. It was like someone just knocked the wind out of me, and I had to pause. "What are you talking about? Would you go this far Michael? Leave me alone."

I walked off the dance floor not knowing where I was going. I needed to catch my breath. This didn't make any sense. Getting married? What? That couldn't be true. Montel was my man. Married to whom? What the fuck was going on around here? I needed answers and Montel was the only one who could give them to me. Just as I walked inside to talk to Michael to ask him where this hotel was, he was on me. Michael tried to calm me down, but there was nothing he could say or do.

"Look, Michael just tell me where the hotel is. I won't believe it unless I see it for myself."

"I'll take you there, but promise me you won't act crazy."

"Done," I said quickly.

I was on fire on the way to the hotel. I felt crazy, out of control. I couldn't be held responsible for my actions. I wasn't thinking. I wasn't thinking about the party, the people, the presents, I left. I wasn't thinking about Raymond's problems with the law. I wasn't thinking about Damon and Lisa. I wasn't even thinking that I might lose my job. Nothing was important. All that mattered were my feelings for Montel. He couldn't have been there. Michael was wrong. He only got one good look at him. This just couldn't be. I was open. My emotions were on my sleeve. I was vulnerable, driven by what I was feeling inside. I wasn't together. The only thought that crossed my mind was a plea. Please don't let it be him, please don't let it be him. I couldn't bear the thought of my world crumbling down. I couldn't grasp my breath. My anxiety was through the roof. Michael looked at me in a weird way.

"Are you all right, you don't look so good?"

"I 'm fine, just keep driving."

"Look maybe this isn't such…"

"What? A good idea? I have to see for myself, Michael, you don't understand. You just don't understand!"

"What? Betrayal? My wife cheated on me when we were married, I cheated on her. We just were not happy with each other, and we kept hurting each other. Finally we let it go. That's what you have to do, let it go."

"Look, Michael, I appreciate your unnecessary advice, but please, you don't know Montel. You think you do. We are happy; we don't want to hurt each other. You just have to be wrong. That's why we're going to the hotel to find out, to prove to you that you are wrong."

"Oh, is that why we're going?"

Now was not the time for his sarcasm. I wasn't concerned with saving face in front of Michael; I was concerned that, in one instant, one second, my happiness was about to be ripped away.

We reached the parking lot of the hotel. It looked empty.

"Look, Sasha, it was a while ago, he probably is not even there."

"There's only one way to find out. You wait here, I'll be back."

"No I'm going with you."

"This is something I have to do on my own. I'm not going to act crazy, just give me the room number."

Michael opened his mouth to argue. I took my finger and silenced him. He couldn't win with me; I don't even know why he tried. This was something I had to do on my own. I heard the words, "Room 224," and I was out like a prowler in the night.

The Double Tree was a very classy place. Only the ballers and ballettes could afford such a place. One night cost like $500 or more for a suite. *Room 224*, that is all I kept saying to myself. *Room 224*. I hopped on the elevator, pressed button 2. Once I got off the elevator, I could hear the music. It wasn't loud, but you knew a party was going on. A thought crossed my mind, *what will I say when I knocked on the door? Hey, is Montel there?* That wouldn't get me through the door. I kept on walking with no plan in hand, I was just going in there, and no one was going to stop me.

I knocked on the door three times. Maybe I needed to bang it with my foot! Just before I placed my boots in the position to kick, a young brother, spacey looking, came to the door.

"Hey, whazzup!" he said.

It was evident this brother drank up all the available alcohol; probably smoked all the weed, and then some. He smelled like Hennessey and smoke! His platinum teeth blinded me. He was big and burly like a wrestler, so big I couldn't see past him. He would have to step aside so I could see what was going on.

"Is the bachelor still here?" I asked

"Oh snap! Yo dawg, you hired another stripper?" He yelled this through the room. The music was so loud I don't think anyone heard, but one dude did.

The other dude said, "Nah, I didn't order another, but the more the merrier!" He came to the door, "Damn, you fine as hell. What's your name?"

I cleared my throat, "Alize," I said with no shame.

"Well hello, Alize, where you been all night? The party's almost over."

I didn't recognize any of these men, it was even better that they didn't recognize me. I played along with this role, like I came up with it. I eased my way inside, quickly scanning the room for familiar faces. No sign of Montel. The room looked pretty empty. The party must have been over. I walked through the room while these two hound dogs chased my tail! The room was dirty, crumbs, blunts, empty glasses and sofa pillows undone. These niggas threw down! Still no sign of Montel. I turned to the two strays, "Where is the bachelor?"

"Oh, are you just here to dance for him?"

I quickly said, "Yeah, I was hired for a private dance, a special dance, if you know what I mean."

They were so blazed they had to watch my lips to understand what I was saying. Their eyes were blood red! All the men in there were blazed, drunk, and surely didn't know what the hell was going on. There was even a dude on the sofa asleep. Passed out.

The big one with the platinum teeth smiled. "Well, if you're looking for the bachelor, he's in the master bedroom."

The big burly one pointed, and I made my way to the master bedroom.

As I kicked my way through the empty bottles, the crumbs, the garbage, I noticed a torn-down banner at the tip of the so-called bachelor's master-bedroom door. I maneuvered it with my foot. It read, "Congrats, Montel!" My heart stop just then, before I could open the door. It didn't matter if I saw him or not, I saw the banner. Still I couldn't believe it. I set myself up for more torture and entered the room. It was dark, the moon shined, the only light coming in. I heard a voice say, "Who is it?" A familiar voice at that. He lay on the bed, hurt from all the alcohol and substances he abused that night. His face was flat down on the bed. I leaned over; I had to see his face. I took my hand and lifted his chin. Still hoping all this was a dream, still hoping there had to be some explanation. There wasn't. The man face down on that bed, the bachelor, my man, the one who claimed he loved me and only me, Montel, was getting married.

The instant our eyes met he jumped up. "Sasha, what are you doing here?"

I silenced him with my finger, the same technique I used to silence Michael. I couldn't speak just then. Words couldn't come out. I felt a pause, nothing moved, and nothing made a sound. I could see Montel talking, moving his lips. I could see his facial expression, the surprise, the amazement, and the fear.

I said nothing. I turned my back to him, to get out of the room. I felt him on me, at my heels. I moved through the trashy room still not speaking. Montel dashed out after me, hot on my trail. I almost made it to the elevator. I felt like a predator was on my tail and I had to make it. I just had to. I reached to push the button. I didn't hear the bell to the elevator ring; I just saw the light. The elevator doors opened. I got in. Montel, I could still see him talking, trying to explain, but I couldn't hear him. I was in shock!

As the elevator door closed, I suddenly got back my hearing, and with my hearing came my voice.

"Listen; just listen to me, Sasha. Before you say anything, I can explain. I wanted to tell you, but I didn't know how. I just found out myself. I know this looks bad, but trust me, this doesn't change how I feel about you."

I looked at him as my eyebrows rose. I knew then, that I was out of control. Before I knew it, my fist balled up and struck Montel in his eye.

He fell back, and began yelling! "What the fuck is wrong with you?!"

"What is wrong with me? You can sit there and try to explain! What are you going to say, how are you going to say it? You are fucking getting married Montel. Married. Not to mention that you are fucking me, not to mention that you are in love with me, not to mention that today is my fucking birthday and you are supposed to be at my party dancing with me! What do you think you can say? You tell me you still love me! Does that word just ooze out of you like diarrhea! You are sick, a sick bastard, and I hope shit never goes right in your life. You bastard!"

I just started hitting him, all my hurt, all my anger, words couldn't express. He tried to block my blows, but there was no one there to hold me. It was just us. He finally wrestled me to the ground. I still kept hitting him. I was yelling at the top of my lungs. "Where were you when I needed you, where were you? Married, Montel. I could take you breaking up with me, but this? You didn't even tell me, you pretended everything was cool!" My face was red, I kept yelling. "How could you do this, what the fuck is wrong with you?"

"Stop hitting me! Just listen."

"Listen to you? That is all I have done for months is listen to you! 'I love you, Sasha; I want to be with you, Sasha. You and me belong together; I want to marry you, Sasha.' That is all you say! You are a liar, a fucking liar!"

He attempted to hold me; I threw his arms off me, "Don't touch me!"

The elevator door opened. I dashed out, Montel still on my heels.

"Sasha would you wait a minute!"

"Get away from me!" I yelled

I caught everyone's attention. I didn't care who knew; I didn't care who saw. "Leave me alone!"

I walked out, with Montel still following, and ran to the parking lot.

"Look damn it, Sasha, she's pregnant!"

That stopped me cold, I turned and looked to him, "What? Is that supposed to be some excuse? Is that supposed to make me feel better? Is that supposed to make it right?"

"It explains this. I was going to tell you, but I didn't know how. I didn't want to ruin what we had; you mean so much to me."

"Shut the fuck up with that shit!"

He tried to hold me, but I pulled away.

"I didn't want it to be this way; it was just one time, one time. That one time changed everything though." Montel shook his head.

I looked at him, thinking *like who are you fooling?*

I cleared my throat. "I could see if you and I had problems that couldn't be worked out. But that is not the case. You have the need to be overly loved because you are overly self-indulged; one woman's love isn't enough for you. You need the love of two. Well I need the love of one man, who sees me and only me. I cannot be shared nor split in half. You can't stand there and tell me this is just a one-time thing. That old feelings crept on your backdoor and you just couldn't resist. You love this. Through my entire time with you, you have always loved the drama; you have always loved the conflict. I don't care if it was one month, two months or three weeks ago; you demolished any chance we had together. I can't continue to believe in your love for me. I can't lie to myself. You will never be mine, always drifted apart from me because I am not enough to satisfy your hunger for love. Bottom line; get another body to love you because I have put this one to rest. Do not call me; write me, or come by my house. We cannot be friends, I love you but I love myself more. I have to move on past this anguish."

"Sasha wait! I, I, I, don't know what to say. I love you. You know that. I could never hurt you intentionally. I, I, you know that I just broke away from my ex and bam, like that, I saw you, and remember all that could have and would have been between us. I don't need two women to love me, I only need you, and I know that now. I know I should have told you what was going on, but I didn't know how; I didn't want to lose you. I wanted to tell you in my own way, not like this. It was months ago, one time with my ex-girlfriend. The week we split up, when you came back from your weekend trip with your girls. I thought we were through. It was one time, a time when I was weak, missing you like crazy. I felt like shit when it was over. I wanted to tell you. I wanted to build this up from the truth and truth only. Please don't walk away from me. I need you. I don't want anyone else, but you. I can't sleep without you next to me. You are the missing piece to my soul. I made a mistake; I am willing to admit that. I never ever wanted to hurt you, that look on your face kills me."

Montel knelt on his knees with his hands placed in prayer form, "Please forgive me. I know it's going to take a while to trust me, but I will earn it. I want you in my life."

I turned away because I didn't want him to see me cry. "I don't know what you are asking me to do?"

Montel took a breath, "I'm asking you to wait for me, don't give up on us. I made a mistake, and now I'm paying for it. I know what it's like to grow up without a father. I don't want that for my child, you know that. Let me do this; let me make this right. I promise, I will do right by you. Know that you are the only one for me. I just have to do this right now; I just hope you can understand."

I couldn't hold it any longer, "Go away, I do not want to hear from you. I can't think clearly with your words, you have to go."

"I'm not going; you are never going to get rid of me because I am part of you. I know you hate me right now, but I'm going to do whatever it takes to make you a part of my life again." Rising from the ground, he wiped away his soft tear. "Sasha, I love you, do you hear me?"

I placed my hands over my ears and turned away.

"I need you. I want you. Hear me baby please I…"

"Leave me alone damn it, I can't take this." I stormed off. Crying the whole way to the car. I stopped and fell to the floor. It was as if I was having a nervous break down. I began to breathe faster and faster. My heart pounded. I tried to raise my legs, but my knees gave way. I tried to pull out my keys, but my hands were shaking. All that came to my mind was, *I love this man, why would he hurt me so? I trusted this man, why would he lie to me? I need this man, I'm empty without him.* Could I forgive him? Could I wait for him? No, that wasn't an option. *Pick yourself up girl, don't let him do this or see you like this.* Words of encouragement were trying to kick in. *I love this man; I don't want to be without him. Don't think that way Sash. He did it before, he will do it again. Why can't I just let go? Because you love him, you trusted him and now he has broken your heart. Your feelings aren't the issue. The issue is what to do next in a relationship that you cherished for so long and now has fallen apart. What is your next move, how will you survive? Can you make it through or will you fold and believe in this relationship?* These were the questions I asked myself.

I finally realized that I couldn't find my keys because I didn't drive. Just then Michael came out of the hotel. "Where were you? I've been looking for you all over."

I couldn't even begin to explain. "Just take me home."

"Are you all right?"

"I'm fine, just take me home."

Michael put me in the car and closed the door. Montel had lied to me for months. On the way home from the hotel, I started putting things together. This was no one-night stand with his ex. They had probably been kicking it the same time we were. Pregnant, married: two things I just couldn't understand. We talked about marriage; we talked about kids. When was he going to tell me? It was like he was living two different lives. He wasn't ever going to tell me, he would rather keep this lie going so he could have his way. Greedy bastard! The audacity to ask me to wait for him, I wasn't waiting for shit! As I followed the yellow and white lines on the highway the thought came to me. Montel and I were over, what was I going to do now?

CHAPTER SIXTEEN

The next morning felt like a hang over. I wasn't drunk but I was hung over on love. My everything just went away. It was as if I was in mourning. Everything seemed to move in slow motion. I was angry and sad inside, all at the same time. I thought Montel loved me, I thought we were building something. I broke every rule I had ever made when it came to men. Montel had me snowed. I would put on the blinders to his imperfections, his wrongs, his unprettiness. I only saw what I wanted to see. Couldn't anyone tell me shit. I knew what I wanted, and that was the end of that.

That morning was one of the worst mornings ever. It felt worst than the morning after my parents died. I was left alone again. Abandoned. Love left me behind. It was different because then I had Raymond; we both were going through it together. Now who did I have? Who knew what I was going through? Raymond had Tasha. T had Ricky. Michelle had Jamal. Lisa had Damon. Tanya had her husband. I'm sure Aunt Mimi had some fella. I was all alone, no one would understand. I had cleared my life of past acquaintances to be with Montel. Now that he was gone, I was left standing alone. Something I hadn't done in a very long time. Something I don't think lasted too long either. This felt like it was going to last forever. When did it get this bad? When did I lose control of me? I hated Montel for doing this to me. Even more, I hated myself for letting him.

It was 11 a.m. and I still was in bed. I didn't want to get out of bed ever. I didn't have to go to work, no job. Nothing to keep me busy. I wanted to cry, but I was too angry. The sun beamed in through the window. I pulled the covers over my head. My belly began to growl. I wouldn't even get out of bed to eat. If I could hold my pee, I wouldn't get out of bed to go to the bathroom either. Life sucked! Just then my phone rang. I thought *who the hell is this? I don't want to talk to anyone!* I reluctantly answered the phone after I let it ring twelve times. It was T.

"Girl I have been trying to reach you all morning. You have to come down to my house, shit is about to get ugly."

I didn't feel like explaining to T that I wasn't coming. I just said no.

"Sasha, you don't understand. Linc done put all my stuff on the lawn. He done changed the locks, and he is serious!"

Still not in the mood for this I said, "I thought you let Linc go, you're with Ricky now."

T began to plead her case, "I was but I never got around to it."

In other words, T was holding on to her spare tire, just in case things with Ricky didn't work out. Something I should have done with Montel. Rule number one; never burn all your bridges. "Well T, what do you expect? You have strung Linc along for years. How long do you think he was going to take it?"

"Whose side are you on?"

Honestly, I was on Linc's side. T had done him so wrong, but how could I explain this to my girl? She didn't understand. She was on the other end of the table spinning the legs, while Linc and I were the ones being spun around. "T, I'm just trying to tell you the facts. Linc is upset with you and tired of your shit. So just pick up your stuff and go about your business."

"Whatever, Sash, I can't go out like this. He has my clothes in garbage bags, my things boxed up, like he's a fucking mover. I can't get into my own house."

"Wait, I thought that was his house?"

"Yeah he bought it fine, but still I decorated it. He just put out my clothes and stuff. I want my other things."

"T just move on. Is that stuff that important?"

"Damn right it is, it is the principle. He can't dump me, I'm dumping him."

"Well why don't you just call him and straighten things out?"

"That jerk done changed the number!"

"Damn T, how long you been gone for him to do all this?"

"Oh just like two days, but I'm saying, I want my stuff!"

I wanted to laugh but I had no energy. "T, what would you like me to do, help you move your stuff?"

"Oh, I can see you got jokes, Ms. Sasha. You better get down here before things start to get out of control and you see me on the news for strangling Linc!" T hung up.

I had no motivation at all to go minutes from my house to T and Linc's crib. I had my own thing that I was going through. I lay in my bed for like twenty minutes. *Oh hell, it's better than lying here thinking about spilled milk.* I got up, got dressed and went down to see what was going on. As I walked out my front door, Michael was out there. I asked him what he was doing there, but I already knew. He had bagels and juice from Dunkin Doughnuts in his hands. How sweet. I grabbed him and the bagels and took him with me to T's house just in case things got out of control.

By the time we got to T's place, Linc was at the window yelling all sorts of names at T. "You slut! It's women like you who give other women a bad name!" Linc had had it
with T.

T, of course, showed no emotion. She kept egging him on, "That's right nigga, I played you before you got a chance to play me. Now stop all this dumb shit and open the fucking door!"

This scene was similar to a TV series. The roles were definitely reversed. Linc was the angry wife, and T was the no-remorse husband. I got out of the car and went over to T. "Girl, stop making a fuss. Get your stuff and go."

"Fuck that, I'm not done with this nigga!"

Linc said, "You better get your girl, Sasha, before something happens to her."

"What, are you threatening me little man? If you are so tough open the door. Changing locks. You afraid of me?"

Linc didn't even answer that taunt.

Michael, like always, came to the rescue. He flashed his badge and said, "Sir, can we just calm down and work this out like adults?"

"Yeah we could if we were dealing with adults. But, you see her right there; she is nothing but a little tramp."

T took off her shoe and threw it at Linc. Linc wasn't fast enough. The shoe hit him in the nose.

He grabbed his nose and said, "You see, this is what I have to deal with officer. I want her off my property now!"

Michael said, "Do you have proof that this is your house?"

Linc said, "I sure do!" gesturing Michael to come to the door.

T followed Michael. He turned around and ordered her to stay right there. Michael went inside and in five minutes came back.

"I'm sorry, T, but you're going to have to leave."

T looked astonished like she couldn't believe it.

I said to Michael, "Well can she at least have her shoe back?" I started smirking, I couldn't hold in my laughter much longer.

T rolled her eyes at me. Michael went in to get her shoe. We helped T put her things in her car. I thanked Michael for his help and told him I would call him later. T and I drove off to my house.

T stayed at my house for a couple of hours and made reservations to stay at one of her suites. I called Michelle and Lisa over for reinforcements because I couldn't handle T on my own. Not today, not after the bullshit I was going through.

T sipped her coffee and began to question Montel's whereabouts. "Where is Montel, I don't want to interrupt anything. Then again, you two don't be sexing anyway, so I guess I'm not interrupting much"

I gave T my cold eyes. She didn't know Montel and I had gotten intimate, nor did she know we were over. "You don't have to worry about Montel. He ain't here, and that is for sure."

T looked at me funny. She knew there was more to what I was saying by the look on my face when I made that last comment.

She began, "What's up is everything all right?"

I said sadly, "Yes, it sure is."

I thought of how all of my friends warned me about Montel, told me something was wrong when we weren't sleeping together. I didn't listen; I couldn't hear them. I definitely wasn't going to feed them this new information, that they were right. Especially, seeing how they all still had a man. I began to think maybe that was the reason it took so long for Montel and me to sleep together. He was with someone else the whole time. To think I believed his stories about wanting to wait, wanting it to be special. He had me so good, so nice and snowed! I believed anything that came out of his mouth.

The doorbell rang. Michelle and Lisa came in with food and drinks. It wasn't even six o'clock and we were about to get wasted on a Sunday evening. We hugged, we laughed, and we ate. I began to get a little up beat, feel a little better about myself. T told her story about Linc kicking her to the curb. I thought I was going to bust a gut, when she told the part about the shoe. The laughter simmered, and the alcohol took effect.

I began to feel confident about telling them about Montel. I cleared my throat, "T is not the only one here with a story to tell. I found out the truth about Montel last night. Before anyone says I told you so, understand you can't tell a woman in love anything. This you all know from experience. Montel is getting married to his ex, who is pregnant, and would like me to wait for him. Experience is what you get when you don't get what you want."

Silence took over for about four seconds.

First T, "What? Well at least you know now before he actually tied the not."

Michelle asked, "Does his fiancé know about you?"

Lisa, T and I looked at Michelle.

I said, "Duh, of course she doesn't!"

"Never mind," Michelle said.

Lisa added, "Fuck him! You got your girls, you got your job, you got everything going for you. He is just another waste; chalk it up as a loss."

"I don't have a job either."

"Excuse me?" T said.

"The other day, I was temporarily suspended; I'm waiting for my hearing to decide my fate."

"Someone pour this girl another glass of Moet," Lisa said as she poured me another glass of champagne.

"Yeah, no job, no man, just me."

Michelle said, "No Sash, you got us, you got your family, you are very talented, and you can do anything, M.D. or not."

Michelle was always like that. If there was a brighter side, she knew what it was. I realized that is how she stayed in her marriage. Her kids were her brighter side, even if Jamal wasn't. I took a good look at Michelle. In a way, I admired her. I always did. She worked hard for her family, for her kids, for herself. Here she is living with HIV, but not letting it destroy her, not letting it end her life, not letting it take control. Where did she get all her strength?

I asked her, "Michelle how can you stay this positive and this strong?"

She said, "Let's just say, I have had the opportunity to look at life and all that I have done wrong and all that I have done right. It has all brought me to this place. I wouldn't change any of that. I love where I am, and who I'm with. My kids are my world; they keep me going. If I didn't have them, I have you guys. Sasha, I have to tell you, what I have already told Lisa and T. I wanted to tell you last because I didn't know how to tell you first. I have HIV. Yes, Jamal. Till death do us part right? I know what you're going to say, but listen, I'm dealing with it. I've been dealing with it for some time now, and I won't say that everything is all right, or that everything will be all right. But I have a lot of hope and life in me, that is what I know for sure."

I hugged Michelle because my tears were taking over. True, I already knew this, but I loved Michelle even more for believing in me, to tell me, to tell all of us. I thought before I had nothing, but I was wrong. I had everything. Everything happened for a reason. I wasn't quite sure what that reason was, but in time, I would know. "How could I have been so sure that Montel and I were meant to be together? If we were, wouldn't we be right?" I looked at T, Michelle and Lisa for answers.

Michelle asked, "Are you going to wait for him?"

Before I could answer, Lisa yelled, "Hell no, she isn't waiting for him."

I exhaled with the insecurity of an eleven-year old, "I really don't know. How can I get over this, see past this?"

"If you let him tell it, he really is sorry and he wants to be with you," T added.

Lisa jumped in, "Of course, he's sorry, probably the sorriest muthafucka on earth. Look, Sash, you don't have to go for that. You are pretty, successful, fun, full of life; you don't need any bullshit from Montel. Just chalk it up as a loss."

"I can't. I have this ache in my heart; it hurts. I never felt like this before. I have broken up with a bunch of boyfriends and none of them felt like this. This really hurts. My feelings were truly into this and now it seems like the pain is never going away. You know how I feel Lisa. Remember when Jake got locked up, you were a mess? Going up there to see him, bringing clothes, money, anything he needed? Knowing how wrong he did you, knowing how he fucked up your life, you still held on to whatever piece of him you could."

Lisa rolled her eyes back to that time. "I was young and dumb and in love. I would have done anything for Jake. When he went to jail and the judge said life, I almost had a break down. Actually I did. I didn't know what to do. I would have twenty dollars in my pocket and put eighteen of it in his canteen, leaving me with enough for bus fair to get home. I was a mess. I didn't have shit. After the IRS decided to take all I had, I went to stripping in nightclubs. It wasn't until social services tried to take my daughter away I woke up, and most people still don't wake up if your child is taken away. I was lucky; I realized my daughter was all I had and that whatever it took I was going to make sure she was cared for. I figured that if Jake and me were meant to be, we would be. I stopped going to see him because he was so negative and discouraging. 'What are you going to do without me, who is going to want you?' he kept saying to me. Visit after visit, you knew there was no end to this. He was sentenced to life, I wasn't. It was his life, not mine. The more time I spent away, the more I realized he wasn't worth it. This man put my life in jeopardy. Come to find out, he had another wife and kid in Atlanta."

"Whatever happened to her Lisa?" I asked,

"I heard she is locked up for like twenty-four years for trafficking with him. That could have been me there. Where would my daughter have been, in a foster home somewhere? Living through that has made me a stronger person and I don't regret anything. I haven't been up to see Jake in over four years, and it feels damn good."

Michelle said, "See, all of us have a plan in life, a purpose that has already been made for us. We may dip in and out, take shortcuts and detours, but no matter what, you are going to end up where you are supposed to be. Like Lisa. Like Jake. Like you Sash. I can't tell you what is going to happen with Montel, but know that if you and him don't make it, you are not meant to be."

Michelle's words sunk in, but I still loved him, I still wanted him.

"So do you think you and Jamal are meant to be?" T cut in.

"T, if I wasn't certain before, I know now. Till death do us part right? I have accepted that this is how it was supposed to be. I never once cheated on Jamal. I was a good wife to him. Did I deserve this? Of course I don't think so. But look where I am. I have HIV and my husband gave it to me. If that isn't a life sentence, I don't know what is. He can't take all the blame though. I looked the other way when he had affairs. I chose to stay with him, even marry him when I knew the kind of man he was."

"Are you angry though?"

"Of course I'm angry. Of course I'm afraid. But what can I do? Go on a rampage? I have kids. I can't change my fate; I was so bitter, full of self-hatred, full of denial. But I keep saying to myself, what about my kids. Jamal, I hate him, but I love him at the same time. It is hard to explain."

"I know," T said. "Rick is so for me, I don't know why, but he is. I can't get him away from me. I know that through your eyes, Michelle, I am doing dirt, but I love him. I'm not sure we belong, I know it. I just need some time to see what my next move is."

"Montel is getting married, how permanent or destined is that?" I interrupted.

Michelle said, "If you don't know now, you will. You will know, Sasha, you will know. Look at the circumstances, though. Montel is marrying his ex-girlfriend that he got pregnant from a one-night stand. Now to me, that doesn't seem like a blissful happy marriage. I give it a year."

We laughed, but I knew it would take longer than that for me to get over Montel or for us to be together.

Changing the subject, I said to Lisa, "So what's up with you and Damon, Lisa?"

"Please that is over."

"He sure did put a smile on your face."

"I know. He was a fresh breath of air too."

"Look Lisa, I'm not the one to give advice. I don't know what Damon's motives were, but if shit was good between you and him, you owe it to yourself to find out if he is that special someone or not."

"I know all this; I am the expert in failed relationships."

"No, I think that would be Sasha," T added.

"Hey, I am in pain here, show some sympathy," I said sadly.

We began laughing. I was so lucky to have them, even if I didn't have Montel.

We sat talking about Michelle and enforcing that we would stay her girls no matter what. I knew all about HIV and how it was transmitted, so I didn't look at Michelle as a threat to me. It would just take some time to adjust to her condition. Things got sad in my house for a while, with talk of what Michelle would like to happen with her kids if anything happened to her. There in my house we cried, and we laughed. There in my house stood four strong women. No matter what men entered our lives, no matter what mistakes we had made in life, no matter what wrongs more than rights were done to us. We still stood with no promise that tomorrow would be any better or any worse, or that there would be any tomorrow. We just hung on to hope that there would be.

CHAPTER SEVENTEEN

The next two months felt like two years. I had not spoken to or seen Montel since that night. He still was in my system though, I still felt for him. The days went by so slowly, the nights felt so lonely. It was such an unfamiliar feeling. As if I was with Montel since birth and now he was torn away from me and I didn't know how to live without him. I still couldn't believe he was getting married. I thought *where was I when all this happened?* It didn't matter where or when, the fact remained, he was gone and I had to move on with my life.

After two months, the hospital still hadn't called for my hearing; I hadn't worked in two long months. I wondered if I still knew how to deliver babies. With no work and no love life, I thought I'd go crazy. The bills started to pile up; my savings had been tapped out by Raymond's case. The D.A. dragged Raymond's case on for a month, all for him to get a slap on the wrist, luckily. He was ordered to do six months of community service and take an anger-management class. That slick-ass lawyer did a very good job of cleaning up the mess. However he wasn't cheap. I got his bill in the mail a week after the case for a whopping $30,000.

What did I do, I couldn't cover it in my savings, so I American Expressed it! Now I am paying that monthly with the interest, plus my car, insurance, house taxes, medical, etc. I had not seen a mall in two months! I was broke like I was in college. Stretching a hundred bucks for a month. These days felt like no end. My pride wouldn't allow me to borrow money from anyone. Besides, Raymond was making contributions. He started paying rent for living upstairs, so that helped out a lot. But I couldn't live like this for long. The bill collectors were calling and I had no answer for them, just the check is in the mail, buddy, wait for it!

I had to do something, so I started substitute teaching like two weeks ago. I taught fifth graders, the most impressionable age to be. I was hesitant at first, but it is kind of fun now. It took a lot of getting used to but I'm making it. It definitely is a step down from the fabulous world of physicians. It was less stressful though; very low and unfamiliar pay as well. I realized in two weeks why teachers were always on strike; they got paid nothing. But working as a teacher definitely wasn't for the money, I knew that much. Anyway if the hospital didn't call me soon, I would be selling the BMW and everything else that was unaffordable. Oh life just couldn't be better, I kept saying to myself. Lately I saw more of the ladies, and more of my Aunt Mimi. Since she and Tanya were the ones to clean up Raymond's mess, she took it upon herself to watch us, like we were kids. She wasn't a bother though, real helpful, my counselor to bad break ups. I would go over to her house for dinner; Raymond and Tasha would come too. We would laugh and talk about old times, our parents, and when we were growing up. They knew about my job status.

I thought Aunt Mimi would scold me, and be so disappointed that I fucked up. She was disappointed, I could tell, but she was more encouraging. As we reminisced about when I was a little girl, she told me how everyone knew I was going to be something; everyone knew I was going to have my name in lights somewhere. I could do anything, she described me that way.

"Sasha Freeman is going to do something special some day, she just doesn't know it, she doesn't realize it. She may try to fight it, and hide from it, but she will not be able to." That's how my mother described me; those were her exact words.

Of course I didn't share her enthusiasm, but I tried to live up to what she knew I would be. I guess that's where becoming a doctor rooted from. I chose something respectable, honorable, highly looked up to. So an obstetrician was the perfect choice. I excelled in high school, college and even medical school. I kept going, as if this path was the one I had chosen.

The more time away from being an obstetrician, the more I began to question my motives to become a doctor. I loved delivering babies that was no question. The look on the parents' faces when that newborn face appeared moved me in indescribable words. I was not fond of the hospital politics and the rules and regulations though. I thought of myself as a liberal. I didn't miss the hospital though. I did miss my patients, and the money of course. But the more time I'd been away, the less it seemed important.

I don't know. I was in a weird place. I doubted myself in every way. I hadn't been on a date, or even pulled a number from a guy when I went out. I felt like a recluse, an outsider, antisocial even.

Aunt Mimi encouraged me to do something, in the meantime, to at least pay the bills. Teaching popped in my head because I liked to teach my new mothers, and enjoyed sharing information when I was a physician. So I decided to substitute the little buggers. I renewed my Lamaze license too. After college I was a Lamaze instructor, but once I went into medical school, I didn't have time anymore. I enjoyed that so much though. So I decided to do that as well.

I was used to working up to fifty hours per week. Now I had so much time on my hands, I didn't know what to do with myself. Sunday dinners at Aunt Mimi's house turned into three nights a week. I volunteered to take Tasha to her doctor's appointments; I even signed her up for my Lamaze class, Michelle too. Their babies were due around the same time. So time was starting to fill in. During the day I would teach, during the night Lamaze classes four times a week.

Another month went by, no word from the hospital board, bills piled up even more. My teaching salary and Lamaze classes would have been sufficient to pay my bills if I didn't live beyond my means. I lived a physician's salary life, not a teacher's, and that started to catch up on me real fast.

Raymond was doing his community service, working two jobs to prepare for his unborn child. Tasha and I became real close in the months she was pregnant. She really loved Raymond, and I was glad he had her in his life. She was no way near as trifling as that Tina. She was sweet, smart and funny. Raymond was real lucky. She didn't have much family though.

They were from New York, and it was just her and her cousin. So I got with her cousin, Marsha, and we planned Tasha a baby shower.

Aunt Mimi, Tanya and her husband, Raymond, Tasha's cousin and Tasha's parents attended. It was nice; they received mostly everything they needed, with the exception of a crib. Raymond and Tasha wanted to pick that out themselves personally. Of course the shower was at my house. It was more of a grown-up shower, not just the women. Tanya's husband was there and Aunt Mimi brought a younger man she had been seeing for about five months now, that was a record. Raymond had Tasha, and Tasha's parents had each other. It was starting to turn into a couple's only party. One I knew I had to cut out of.

The doorbell rang. To an unexpected surprise, it was Detective Perry. He had dropped by from time to time, so called checking on Raymond to make sure he was going to his anger management classes and such. I guess that was his punishment from the D.A. for him helping Raymond out. He was assigned to baby-sit Raymond.

Because I had two Alabama Slamas that I made myself, I started my regular comments to Michael. "What are you doing here; did I forget to pay you, babysitter?"

Michael chuckled, "No for your information Ms. Sasha, I was invited."

He stepped in the doorway without me moving or inviting him in like he owned the place. He yelled out a hello to everyone, and turned his attention toward me. He took one look at me, as I was swaying left to right with my third cup of Alabama Slama in my hand.

I was about to lash out another smart comment, when he took my cup and said, "I think you've had enough of that, Miss."

I was astonished. Who did he think he was coming in my home, telling me what to do? "Whatever, I'll just get another. What are you drinking Detective?"

He leaned in to reach my ear and said in a very sexy voice, "How many times do I have to tell you, Miss Sasha, call me Michael."

I don't know if it was the drinks, or the fact that I hadn't been done in three months, but with those words, I got very hot. I switched my hips in the kitchen to pour me another cup and cool off.

Of course, giving me no space, Michael came into the kitchen to lecture me on drinking. "You really should slow down on the drinks, it isn't attractive."

Me being tipsy let no words be thought out, just feelings. "Look Michael, you may think you know me, but you don't. I'm grown, and very capable of taking care of myself. Oh, and I know what is attractive and what isn't, and trust there is no one at this family gathering I'm trying to attract."

Michael bent his head back, and rolled his eyes. "You are always taking my concern for something else. I'm not trying to tell you what to do; I am just worried about you."

I looked at him in disgust. "Worried? What do you have to be worried about? This is a party. If you haven't noticed, everyone is drinking, everyone is having a good time. Why don't you have a good time, and stop being so worried about me!"

"Why are you always pushing me away?"

"Why are you always pushing up on me?"

"Because I..." Michael didn't finish his sentence. He stopped, as if he was about to say something but wasn't sure how to put it.

"Look do you want something to drink or not?"

"Yeah, pour me whatever you're having."

"That would be an Alabama Slama, Detective. Watch it now, it might creep up on you."

"Yeah I know how that can happen."

I wasn't sure if he was talking about the drinks or something else. I ignored it, and went to be the host for the party. We laughed and ate, talked about old times. Aunt Mimi even brought out a baby picture of Raymond, trying to figure out what this baby would look like. Of course Tasha's parents proclaimed they had the dominant features in the family, but it was just playful antics, nothing serious. Her parents seemed very cool; they seemed to like Raymond a lot. Of course, they pushed the issue of marriage.

Tasha's father, Mr. James Anderson said, "Well, when are you kids getting married? This baby is coming soon, you know."

Raymond clammed up. Tasha said, "We're getting married after the baby is born."

I looked a bit surprised, so did Raymond. I didn't know about this. Raymond just nodded and smiled. Her father and mother looked very pleased with this news and moved on to the next subject. I thought this marriage announcement was not planned nor agreed upon by both parties. I didn't even see a ring on Tasha's finger. I would have to question this later.

I began to clean up as everyone started leaving. Tanya had to be in court tomorrow and her husband was going out of town. I thought of them as the perfect couple, I always had. They started dating back in high school; I even remember when they met. He was going with one of Tanya's girls' girl. Tammy as a matter of fact, it was her friend Diedra. Tanya and Larry were just friends though. The next thing I knew they were together, and Tanya got a phone call from Diedra and accused Tanya of stealing her boyfriend. Tanya was blunt with the girl. Tanya told her that she wasn't treating him right anyway, and they had gotten together after him and her broke up, so that was that. I didn't think it would last; I looked at it as Tanya was Larry's rebound. But I was so wrong, because look at them now. Years later still together, married. They were my ideal couple, full of happiness and love. I just knew I would have the same thing. Montel crept in my mind like always. He stayed in my mind on a daily basis. The what ifs, and could of beens were all I thought about sometimes. Montel and I started off as friends, why didn't we work?

Anyways, I finished cleaning up with Aunt Mimi's help. As she began to leave she said, "Why do you act like that towards that man?"

I was confused, "What man?"

"That fine Detective, he has got it bad for you and you treat him so wrong."

"What!" I said with a look of astonishment. The same look I gave her when she figured out I was lying, trying to go somewhere I was told not to go.

Aunt Mimi put her hands on my shoulder, "Girl you just don't know when to open your eyes, do you?"

She left me with that thought. I started a fire and turned on the TV to watch a movie. I was no way near tired, and I was very much up. The alcohol began to wear off, and I was left thinking about Montel. I also tried to rationalize Aunt Mimi's comment. I didn't know how to open my eyes. Did that mean I let Montel trick me into loving him and only him, or worse, I didn't know how to pick men? That thought scared me.

After all this time, I still didn't get it right. I was by myself, alone, watching a movie. I had dated a ton of men, wasted a lot of fingers, and wasted a lot of time. But I never questioned myself; I never thought that I was the reason things didn't work out. I mean, like Jason, how did I know he was crazy. He was the problem not me. I started going over all my relationships in the past, and I began to realize, damn it, maybe I am the problem, I just don't know how to pick them, I look for the wrong things. Therefore, I end up being done wrong. I think to play it safe, from now on, I will not pick them, I will let them pick me, and see what happens.

As I devised a new dating plan, my doorbell rang. I thought, *who the hell is this?*

The door opened. Michael entered, saying nothing. He looked peculiar, like he was on a mission or something.

I said, "Can I help you, did you lose something, forget something, what?"

He paced my living room floor for about a minute, still saying nothing.

I shut the door and said, "Hello, do you hear me talking in that thick skull of yours?"

He looked at me and walked up to me swiftly. Before I knew it, he grabbed my face and kissed me. I felt that kiss forever. It was so sensual and endearing, I wanted more. He stopped and looked at me in the eyes.

He said, "I wanted to do that from the first day I saw you. All this time, I fought it; I fought what I felt, and how I felt because I was afraid. I still am, but I feel like, if I don't kiss you, if I don't tell you this, I will regret it for the rest of my life."

I knew what Michael was saying, I knew what Michael was feeling, I had felt it too, but it was so forbidden. I had been secretly attracted to Michael, but I hid it with the snide comments and rudeness to each other that we shared. Did I do that because I was afraid of how I felt?

I didn't know the answer to that, but I knew what my next step was. I kissed him back without saying a word. I began to undo his coat, undo his sweater. I kicked off my shoes and he kicked off his shoes. I unbuckled his belt, then his pants. He pulled off my dress over my head. He kissed my neck. My nipples rippled. I felt his hardness against my belly. I grabbed it and caressed it with my hand. He sucked on my lips, then my chin. I moaned. He kissed my neck again, then moved to suck my breast like a lollypop. He pulled me to the floor. My body became submissive to him, following his every motion in sequence. I licked his belly all the way up to his neck. His hands grabbed the back of my neck, and then he grabbed my hair. He turned me over to my back and licked me, first down, then up. I kissed him as his fingers ran through my privates. His fingers touched me, and I moaned as my tongue was down his throat. I heard the tearing of a condom open. He slid it on and then slid inside of me. I moved up and down riding him. He lifted me up and slammed me down on the sofa where he could control the strokes. He kissed my breast as he thrusted inside of me softly. No thoughts entered my mind, just feelings, emotions. The sweat from our bodies soaked my pillows. I grabbed the ends of the sofa; Michael lifted my legs over his shoulders. I bit my lip as I tried not to scream. He moaned and kissed my lips. As I reached my point, I buried my face in his neck. He began to thrust faster and harder. He pinned my hands down as he came. His body collapsed onto mine, as he kissed my neck and then my lips. We lay there for a moment, silent. I didn't know what to say; I don't think he did either. As the silence filled up the room, I closed my eyes.

A moment later, I felt Michael lift from my shoulder and he said in a playful voice, "What, I know you are not falling asleep on me?"

I smiled, and kissed him. We continued this affair upstairs in my bedroom with no fear, no regrets; just a whole lot of fun. We didn't know where this was going and neither of us wanted it to end. We just carried on like tomorrow didn't matter. This time was our time, and that is all that did matter

CHAPTER EIGHTEEN

The next day, Michael got up and ran me a bath. He scrubbed my back and I scrubbed his. I asked him did he want to know where the donut shop was for breakfast; he asked me did I know how to turn on a stove. We continued with playful little smart-ass remarks, as if nothing changed. He told me he would call me later; I knew he would.

I didn't know what just happened though. We were always bumping heads, at each other's throat. What were we going to be now? I didn't have the answer and neither did he. I was just going with the flow, letting the chips fall where they may. I did like Michael. He definitely grew on me. I just didn't know if what we had would go any further than it already had. I sat trying to convince myself that this was more than a fling, more than a rebound type thing.

After pondering and pondering, I just gave up and said fuck it. It will be whatever we make it be. One thing was for sure, we had to put the comments aside so we both could decide what our next move was. As far as I was concerned Michael turned my little ass out, therefore the relationship we had grown into was definitely something to look into.

I went to teach that morning and afternoon. I was feeling good, no grouch in this body. I was glowing. I couldn't believe it. I had been feeling so down, so unwanted lately; it felt good to feel alive again. I gave no homework assignment, just to catch up on their reading if they hadn't. I went home, Michael called, like he said. He wanted to meet up before I went to Lamaze class. We went out for some buffalo wings at Pizzeria Uno near the center where my class was. The plan now was for him to pick me up after Lamaze class. I must have put it on him, cause he couldn't get enough of me. We started the smart comment routine over dinner. The atmosphere felt comfortable, almost like I was out having dinner with the ladies. We had just about talked about everything except us. I knew that subject was about to come up though.

"What time is your class over?"

"Oh like around 9 p.m."

"That's good; I should be off by then to pick you up, can't have my lady out too late by herself."

"Your lady?" I said with curiosity.

"Yeah, you're my lady, my home girl, my buddy."

"I see. Well, as I recall, you refer to me as a man-eater, so why would you want me to be all of this to you if you think of me that way?"

"And as I recall, you told me that I have nothing better to do than to bother women I can't have."

"So you think you have me now?"

"Look, before this gets into a debate or a heated argument, let me just say that last night wasn't a fling or just some one night thing. I have been trying to get at you for some time now, but you always seem preoccupied. When I first met you, I thought you were blown. Always having a brother hemmed up, love sick over you, that's why I didn't bother. I didn't want that brother to be me. But it was no coincidence why I kept coming around. I was drawn to you Sasha, but I didn't want to get hurt by you. After my first wife, I was never going to let pretty faces be my objective to pursue a relationship. Some of you women with these faces think you can get a guy to do just about anything which is true, but I didn't want to be that guy anymore, motivated by the beauty I saw outside a person, not inside. So, I began to date six or seven pieces and left dime women alone. I let that control my whole thought process on meeting someone. The pretty women will hurt you, but the not-so-pretty ones will worship you."

I tried to interrupt, but Michael held his hand up and motioned me to wait.

"It wasn't until I met you that I realized that whole thought process was stupid. Not every pretty face will treat a brother like shit, and not every pretty woman sees herself like some sort of goddess that needs to be worshipped. In fact a lot of pretty women are insecure. Anyway, I tried to deny my feelings for you for a very long time, but the more I'm around you, the more I can't keep away from you. You have a big heart and a lot of courage, that's what I like most about you, and I feel like we have a lot to make something between us work. I care a lot about you Sasha, and I'm trying to be with you, but I don't know what you want. But I'm damn sure going to try because I will not forgive myself if I let you go so easily without knowing how I feel."

I sat back like, wow that sure was an ear full. I didn't now how I was feeling about Michael. The attraction was there. I cared about him. We were definitely good friends who could lean on each other. I didn't know if I wanted to be with him like that though. I didn't even know if I was ready for a relationship.

"Look Michael, you're right. I'm not so sure that this is the right time for me to be getting involved like that. I do care about you and I do love it when you're around, no matter how much I try to push you away. But I just don't know if I'm ready for all that, and I don't want to leave you hanging. But I don't want to rush into something just because it feels right. You understand what I am saying?"

"Of course, and I'm not trying to push you anywhere you don't want to go. But I feel for you, and that's something I can't ignore. So what do you want to do?"

As if I really had an answer for him, right now. "I just want to take things super slow. I want to continue being friends with you no matter what. I'd like to keep you in my life, no matter what. I guess what I am saying is, I'd like to try to see where this is going. So we can be homey lover friends. How does that sound?"

"If I am not mistaking you want to just kick it."

"Exactly, exactly. Is that cool with you?"

"Yeah, that's straight with me."

There, it was settled. Michael and I were kicking it. We were not obligated to one another, meaning we could see other people, but it was understood that we were trying to build something together. This was different from what I had with Damon, because with us, it was all about sex. With Michael, it didn't have to be about sex. We could see each other, go hang out, and not just have sex or call each other when we were horny. If sex came into play, it just did, but we both understood that this was not just a booty-call relationship. I didn't know how else to describe it, to make it sound good. We were not together as boyfriend and girlfriend, no titles, we were just friends.

Michael dropped me off at my Lamaze class. I taught four nights a week, Monday through Thursday from 7 p.m.-9 p.m. I had about six to ten mothers in each session. Some came once a week, some came twice a week, and some came four times a week. It all depended on their bankroll. Health insurance did not cover Lamaze classes. I charged $300 a person for two nights a week for a four-week session. If a person wanted to come four nights instead of just two, I charged $200 for the extra days for a four-week session. I thought that was pretty reasonable for my time and effort. My prices were pretty good compared to others. Since I still had some associates at the hospital, they recommended their patients to me, so my little sessions were beginning to pay off.

This was a brand-new class, which was full consisting of ten clients. If the referrals kept coming in like this, then I wouldn't need to teach; I could do this full time. But then again, it all depended on how many people signed up. I couldn't very well plan my monthly salary if I didn't know how many clients I had for that month. It was an idea to keep in mind if my license was actually taken away over something as trivial as what Dr. Roebuck was accusing me of. Yeah, I did it, but damn I'm a young eager doctor. I didn't put any patients at risk, so I don't see why this is such a big deal. Anyway, my clients began to flow in. Michelle and Tasha of course received a discount for my class, they were the first two in. Raymond had to work and Jamal was not around, so Lisa came with Michelle, and Aunt Mimi came with Tasha. We sat around chatting, waiting for the other eight clients to arrive. Aunt Mimi said, "You have got a kicker on you Tasha. Why didn't you guys figure out what the sex of the baby was?"

"Oh we didn't feel like it, we wanted it to be a surprise. Raymond talks of a boy all the time, and it really doesn't matter to me, so I just say whatever," Tasha replied.

"Yeah, Raymond has high hopes for a boy. I am sure though, he will love the baby no matter what sex it is though. He's so excited Tasha," I added.

Aunt Mimi said, "Now you have yourself a good, hard-working man. He loves you and this baby a lot, and would do anything for you, just remember that honey."

"Oh, and this wedding, why didn't you tell me, Tasha? I didn't know you guys were getting married. I figured if you were, you would have already before the baby was born," I said

"That was my fault; I didn't want to walk down the aisle all fat and not attractive."

"Girl pregnancy is a beautiful thing." Michelle added. "I did wait after my first son to marry his father though, so it is really up to what you guys want to do and so forth. There are no rules."

Tasha agreed. "Plus, with that case Raymond had and him starting his new job and all, we just couldn't afford it."

"What about your parents?" I asked.

"Come on, I'm nineteen-years-old, pregnant, I couldn't ask them to pay for my wedding."

"Why not? That's what fathers are supposed to do." I said.

"No rules, remember," Michelle added.

"Whatever," I said. "I just thought, since your father was pushing marriage so much, he would want to pay for it."

Aunt Mimi interrupted, "Well it doesn't matter. You two love each other, you are good with each other, a piece of paper isn't going to change that. So if you don't have the money for the wedding now, you will have it one day, and you can get married then."

"Yeah, I know. I just wanted to be married before my child realized his parents don't have the same last name, that's all."

I got the feeling from Tasha that there was more to it than that. The more she went on, the more it sounded like to me she wanted us to pay for the wedding. I don't know, maybe I was just jumping to conclusions.

The classroom began to fill up; all nine couples were there except one. I checked off my list. Jennifer Hayes was the missing client. The class started at 7 p.m. and it was 7 on the dot. I couldn't let one client make everyone else late so I started the class. I introduced myself and my background. A lot of the women were pleased that an obstetrician was teaching the class. I went around the room to let them introduce themselves. Most of the clients were twenty-eight to thirty-six-year-old white females, first baby, and very anxious about the birth. Michelle and Tasha were among the youngest. Just as I was about to begin the session, my late client arrived. She was about my height, look the same age as me, light skinned, like me, with long brown hair and hazel eyes. She wobbled in with her obviously-pregnant belly and began to excuse herself for being late.

"I am so sorry I am late. My husband has no track of time, and claims I don't. He thought the class was over somewhere else and started at 6 p.m. Come to find out he doesn't have a sense of direction either, but hey, I love him."

She was cute, a little silly even. "Okay, well I'm Sasha Freeman, I'm the instructor for the class, just come right on in."

I quickly went around the room and gave everyone's names, and began to start the session again. "You said your husband is with you?"

"Yeah, here he comes; he just had to park the car."

Jennifer went to sit on a pillow, as her husband came into the doorway. His light skin chinky eyes and six-foot frame almost knocked the wind out of me. His face was all too familiar, all too knowing. Montel stood in the doorway, not so sure he should enter. He looked at me, as I looked at him. Time seemed to have stopped.

My heart thumped, I stuttered, "Well come on in and join us, Mr. Hayes."

Montel, not sure so sure of what he walked into, found his wife Jennifer and sat with her.

The session is supposed to last for two hours, however it felt like eternity. I ran over the material I had too fast, and the time went nowhere. After realizing that I had finished my session at 8:05pm. I let everyone take a break. I went out of the room to grab some water. Lisa and Michelle came after me.

Michelle hugged me. "Are you going to be alright, Sasha? I couldn't have done in there what you just did. I mean, the nerve of that asshole."

"I know, but I'm sure he didn't know that I was running this class. I haven't spoke to him in three months."

Lisa said, "Still, he should have thought of some way to get him and that dippy girl out of here."

I laughed. "She is kind of dippy, huh?"

"Yeah, girl, she is definitely a bad copy of you. I mean look at her; you are so much cuter, so much prettier," Lisa validated.

Lisa was my girl. I knew none of that mattered. She had him. She was Montel's wife. I couldn't compete with that. Those were my shoes she was stepping in. I couldn't believe it. Out of all the places in this world to see him and his wife, they have to be here. I just don't know how I'm going to get through the rest of this night. *Shit, how am I going to get though the rest of these eight sessions that I have to do with them? Oh this is not going to do.*

"Well, she obviously doesn't know about you, or else she wouldn't be so damn cheerful." Lisa claimed.

We laughed.

"Oh where is T when I need her? This is her thing to do, dealing with the ex and his new wife."

"No honey, you should be glad T isn't here. She would have blown up Montel's spot and you don't need that in front of all these clients," Lisa said.

"You're right. Let me just get through the last forty-five minutes and figure out how I'm going to deal with this."

"We got your back, you know that," Lisa said.

"I know, I'm so glad you two are here. I couldn't face this on my own."

I hugged them as my Aunt Mimi came out. "Is everything all right?" she asked.

"Yeah, lets get this class over with."

"Sasha, is that who I think it is?"

"Yes, Aunt Mimi, let's just finish this up and talk about it later."

I grabbed her by the arm to come inside. I could feel Montel's eyes watching me, wondering what I was going to do next. The boy has no shame, staring at me while his wife has her back turned. "Oh no. You do not need someone like that in your life. No matter how fine he is, he is a dog with a capital D. Leave him alone, Sasha, be the bigger person."

All that Aunt Mimi said made sense; I was just trying to get my bearings. I started the class again. Since I didn't have any more material to discuss for that night, I figured what better way to pass the time than letting the people discuss their concerns and ask any questions they had. Everyone seemed so receptive seeing how I was an obstetrician and could get my expert information as well as Lamaze teaching all in one. I answered question after question and began to feel a little relaxed because I was so emerged into my element. I loved teaching new mothers. I loved the exchange of information. The session was going really well, everyone seemed really into it, I felt they were getting their money's worth. I almost got through the night.

With five minutes to go, I was about to close up the session, when Jennifer decided to ask the final question of the evening. I hadn't heard anything from her all night except her husband this, her husband that. That's all that seem to come out of her mouth. She was really annoying. Her question had something to do with the pain of labor and techniques to soothe the discomfort. I thought, *this is why you're taking Lamaze, dumb ass.* Anyway, I answered her simple question and ended the session. If I had to go through another night with her and him, I didn't know what would come out of my mouth. Montel couldn't have gotten out of there faster. He dragged poor Jennifer out of there by the arm. I know he couldn't stand it, but what could he do? I just hoped he would convince her not to come back to this class with his ass, cause I might not be so friendly next time.

The girls and I went out for a drink. Aunt Mimi went home and took Tasha with her. Lisa called up T to meet us at Unos for a double dose of Pina Colada's and Pearl Harbors. I called Michael and told him of my plans. He seemed cool about it and asked me to call him later.

"Damn, you got a new man already?" Lisa said.

"See that's what I'm talking about. Don't sit around moping, find you another young handsome brother." T and Lisa slapped hands. These two were just wanted I needed.

Michelle asked, "Who is this new fella?"

"Okay ladies brace yourselves, do you remember, Detective Perry?"

"Yeah girl, I remember him," Lisa answered.

"Well, we're trying to do our thing now."

"What!" Lisa's mouth dropped.

"I knew he had a thing for you" Michelle said. "He's a good brother, seems real nice. Don't let this one go."

"I know. We bicker like cats and dogs, but I guess opposites do attract and he is fun to be around."

"Oh, stop trying to convince yourself, Sash. You've been attracted to him from jump, you just be playing yourself with Montel," T interjected.

"True, but I don't want him to be a rebound type, you know. Besides, I wouldn't know a good guy if he smacked me in the face. I just don't know how to pick them, I think. I know what I don't want, but I don't know what I do want. You know. I like Mike, but I feel closure has not happened for Montel and me yet."

"Oh, please! Close that book while you're ahead. Don't play yourself any longer," Lisa demanded.

"Enough about me. Did you and Damon make up, Lisa?"

"That man has been ringing my phone for weeks. After not returning one call, he shows up at my daughter's school, knowing I would be picking her up. He has flowers for me, a Barbie doll for her, and some lame excuse. He said he had to see me and that we needed to talk."

"So did you fall for it?" I asked.

"Of course she did," T said.

"After hours and hours of discussion we came to an agreement."

"In other words, you dropped the panties!" T said

We started laughing.

"Whatever," Lisa said, "I can't hold out too long. I feel funny talking about Damon around you, Sasha, you two were together in all."

"I know. From now on just an update on your progress, no details please!"

"I hear that!" Lisa agreed. "It is so funny, I never thought I could talk to someone one of my girls had been with. That was a rule."

"Yeah, well one, you didn't know about it, and two, when your feelings are into it like that, the rules do not apply," I claimed.

"True!" Lisa agreed.

I never would talk to one of my girlfriends' leftovers, but with such a scarce population of good men, who was I to be picky these days. "Just let me know if it gets serious or not, Lisa, and if it doesn't work out, it just doesn't."

"I know girl, I know."

We sat and talked about new relationships and failed relationships. Our conversations always seemed to be about men, gossip, money and family. I didn't mind though; I enjoyed our conversations. They kept my mind off the other things on my mind right now like Montel. The way he looked, the way he smelled, how jealous I was that he actually got married and is having a baby. That was supposed to be me. We were supposed to be together. I thought *how long can he live this lie? How long can he pretend that what he feels for me is just a thing of the past? Can he truly move on or is he just trying to spare my feelings because he knows he'll hurt me in the end?* I didn't have the answers to these questions, and there was only one way to get the answers and the closure that I needed. I had to call him.

On the way home I thought about what I would say to him once I called. I thought, did he have the same beeper number? What would I do? Should I leave a message and enter my phone number? Oh this was such a bad idea. I didn't know what to do. On one hand, he is the one who destroyed our relationship; he should be trying to make it better. And on the other hand, I still loved him, and in the back of my mind wished things could have been different. Wished things had worked out, if only we had another chance. After all, Montel was my first true love. I thought he meant everything to me. I vowed once that I would do anything to stay with him. Things were so messed up though. I didn't know what to do. Once I got home I just stared at the phone, deciding to call or not to call. I was supposed to be moving on, why couldn't I? I had Michael, Montel had is wife. We should just leave it at that. I decided not to call. I could talk myself into just about anything. I talked myself into not calling Montel.

I jumped in the bath and let my body soak. Oils and bubbles were just what I needed. I kept thinking *this is all for the best. We shouldn't be together, just move on, sister girl. Move on.* After an hour of relaxation and a self-pep talk about keeping my distance from Montel and focusing on Michael, I crept downstairs to get a snack before I fell asleep.

My living room was dark; the only light that shined in was the one from my porch light. I looked outside, as if I was expecting someone. I noticed Raymond's car in the driveway, so I turned off the porch light. As I began to walk upstairs, I noticed a flashing red light in my living room. It was the answering machine. I had messages. I must have looked over them. Too busy pondering about Montel, I went right upstairs and didn't even check my machine. I pressed the button. The first message was at 1 p.m. "Hello, Dr. Freeman, this is Dr. Westgate, from General Hospital.

We have come across your file and have set up a time and date for your hearing. Please give me a call at 617-555-9990, so we can discuss this matter." The next message was received at 11:50 p.m. "Hey, it's me. It was real awkward seeing you today. I hope I didn't cause you any pain. I honestly didn't know it was you who was teaching the class. I basically don't know what's going on in your life anyhow. I just thought I would call you. I don't know, everything is so out of control; I don't even know how it got to this point. Well look, call me when you get this, I really need to talk with you. Alright, bye."

In the background of that message, I heard a women's voice saying, "Montel," as if his call woke her. There it was, my future as a physician and my future with Montel, all in the same night. Two things I was not ready to face.

CHAPTER NINETEEN

I agonized over that phone call for hours. The hours turned to days and the days turned to weeks. I did not pick up the phone to call Montel. I couldn't. I didn't know what to say or what would happen if I did call. However, I did call Dr. Westgate back. My hearing was in three weeks. Dr. Westgate went over all the particulars. I could have co-workers write personal recommendations, anything to make me look good. I could even hire a lawyer if I wanted to. I didn't feel the need to. I went over my case in my mind, and after all the complaining and moaning I did when I was suspended, I realized that it was my fault. I broke patient confidentiality. I broke the rules. If I didn't want to follow the rules, I should have never become a physician. I over stepped my boundaries. I was ready to face my fate. I decided to tell the truth about my actions. Whatever happens next just happens.

My hearing was on a Monday morning at 8a.m. Of course, I was dressed to impress in my Ann Taylor navy blue pants suit with my yellow silk blouse, yellow socks, and navy blue Enzo's penny loafers. My hair was down. I had been wearing it straight in a wrap for a while now. I had butterflies in my stomach the entire morning. Michael stayed over last night. He really was there for me like a real friend. He made me breakfast and wanted to drive me to the hospital. I wanted to go alone. I needed to do this alone. Michael tried to encourage me during breakfast. "So when you start practicing again, you won't have as much free time as usual, will you?"

"Oh stop, I don't know how this is going to turn out. I appreciate you trying to cheer me up but I did the dirt, so now I have to face it."

Michael had a very surprised look on his face.

"What is that look all about?" I asked.

"Well, you've always taken the high road. Even when you're wrong, you never admit it. I have to tell you that you've changed a lot from the first time I met you. You seemed more defensive and righteous then."

"What can I say Michael? I have to open my eyes sometimes, especially when I'm looking at myself."

"Wow!" he said in amazement. "I grow to like you more and more everyday. I admire your strength and courage. You really are woman enough, even at your weakest moment."

"I assume you're talking about Montel."

Michael's eyebrow rose a little. "What ever happen to him? You don't talk much about him."

"That's because I don't have much to say about him. He hurt me, I moved on. He got married, I moved on. He's having a baby. I moved on."

"I know all that. On the outside you seem over it, you seem through with him. But I don't know how you feel on the inside about him, talk to me."

Damn it, why did he have to go and bring up Montel? No, I wasn't over him, I still thought about him every day! Little did

Michael know, I was contemplating calling him. Oh what could I say to get out of this conversation?

"Look, Michael, there is nothing to talk about. Yes, I was in love with that man for a long time, but I know what type of man he is now, and I don't need that in my life. Besides, you do a pretty good job of occupying my time. Why would I want to think about anyone else?"

I placed my hands on his face and gave him a soft kiss to his lips. I gave him that look that he couldn't resist. He was putty in my hands. At least I thought so. Anyway, he dropped the subject and proceeded to finish breakfast.

He kissed me on my forehead instead of my lips when he left. I guess that meant he wasn't pleased with my behavior. Oh well, I thought *Who needs men anyway? They're just driving me crazy. Here I have Montel calling me, then Michael wants to go deeper into our relationship*. It was all too much for me to handle. Maybe a sane person would know what to do, but I didn't.

I made my way to the hospital. Even though in a few minutes my fate as a doctor was about to be decided, I was kind of nonchalant about the whole thing. I felt detached. I kept weighing the pros and cons. Whatever! I just wanted to get this part of my life over with so I could find out what my next move was. I decided long before the hearing that I would tell my story and if they decided to welcome me back, I would go back. If they decided to dismiss me, I would accept that too.

I was one hour early for the hearing. I had to get my bearings. That hour seem to drag. As the time came near, I began to see a couple of familiar faces. Tammy, the back-stabbing bitch, went into the room. Dr. Roebuck managed to crawl her creepy self out from her rock and appear as well. A few others went inside. It must have been the Director of the hospital, the Chief of Staff, Dr. Westgate, and the Director of Occupational Affairs. All of them went in without saying a word to me, just a look of snobbishism, and do rights. I felt like saying, "Fuck you all!" But I was a physician, a professional; I didn't need to make a scene.

It had been like four months. Four long months of them dragging this on. Why couldn't we have had this trial months ago? Why keep me out of work for so long without pay? The more I thought about it, the angrier I got. These bastards were trying to shaft me! I gave them the ammunition to do it. One mistake, one false move and they were ready to kick me out the door. As my rage began to boil, I thought of all the other things I had going for myself and all the other things I had to be grateful for.

Dr. Westgate came into the corridor where I was sitting and signaled me to come in. I went into the dark room feeling confident, unafraid, and ready for my fate. I sat down and crossed my legs as well as my hands. The directors of the hospital stared at me for about two minutes and began the proceedings.

"Dr. Freeman, do you understand the accusations and reasons for this hearing?" Dr. Westgate said.

I nodded.

"Then let's begin. I have heard a signed affidavit from Tamela Jones and Dr. Roebuck, that you underhandedly broke the policy of patient confidentiality. I also have a form that you signed, pertaining to the disclosure of all patient information and how it should be used in this hospital. We have heard from Tamela Jones and Dr. Roebuck, now we would like to hear from you."

One of the directors of the hospital board gave me the okay to speak. I cleared my throat and began to tell my side of the story. I started off saying that I did willingly break patient confidentiality, and was sorry for it. I went on to say, that I meant no harm and that it will never happen again. I went to say that I take full responsibility for my actions and accept whatever might come to me. I had no excuse for my actions, except that I was worried about a friend. Still, that was no excuse for what I did and I had learned from my mistakes. I tried to say all this as sincerely as possible . Whether they bought it or not, suddenly I didn't care.

They looked at one another and wrote a little something on their papers. Dr. Westgate then turned to me and said; "We have decided to let you go this time with a warning."

I said, "Thank you."

He then put his hand up and said, "I am not finished Dr. Freeman. Although the nature of your actions did not bring any harm to this hospital, they were still against hospital policy. We would like to reinstate you at this hospital with a few restrictions. First you will have Dr. Roebuck sign all the prescriptions you write. You will work with Dr. Roebuck when admitting, treating, and discharging patients. We have also moved your office to the fifth floor, so Dr. Roebuck and you can work closer together. And of course there are some other few gray areas about your salary, but you can go over that with human resources."

Just as I thought, I was getting the shaft! Dr. Westgate said it first. My crime didn't cause any harm, not even worth all this, not worth all the aggravation. That vengeful Dr. Roebuck, she was going to make my life hell. She did this on purpose. She wanted me to work with her so she could be my babysitter. And what the fuck was the deal with my pay! This hospital really didn't know whom they were dealing with.

I said, "Well as pleasant as that offer sounds, I will have to decline. I didn't go to four years of college, four years of medical school and three years of residency to be watched like a neonate. Since my license has not been taken away, I will find work elsewhere, because this I must say, is unacceptable. I am not giving Dr. Roebuck the satisfaction of treating me like she did in med school."

"Dr. Freeman, you do understand that you have not finished your fellowship contract with this hospital and that you would have to start all over anywhere else!"

"I completely understand, Dr. Westgate, but in all this time that I have been away, I had a chance to realize that this is not the work I was meant to do. I don't know what that is but this isn't it. I want to help people, not hinder them. With all these rules and regulations and insurance this and payment that, I am not so sure I am helping. I hope you understand."

It was one thing to put up with the politics of how a hospital is run, but to have to put up with Dr. Roebuck was an entirely different story. I just can't do it. I left that boardroom not knowing what my future held for me, but I knew it wasn't as a doctor. I thought maybe they wanted me to self terminate. If so, I would have done it without their help. I've been feeling this way for a while, I just never had the time to really look at myself and what was going on in my life. Now I did.

I passed by Tammy's trifling self. I stopped her and said, "What you did, Tammy, just reminds me of what a sneaky little bitch you really are. But not to worry, unlike yourself, I have no intention of going back on what I said. In the whole scheme of things, your type of people always get what they deserve. If you don't know it now, you will know it soon, make peace with all your wrong doings because your time is definitely near."

I left Tammy with those words, and called Michael to meet me for a drink at Cathay Pacific. I was in desperate need of a scorpion bowl and some shrimp fried rice. I remember Montel took me there a few times. We would drink at least two scorpion bowls and drift off into each other's conversation. I tried to keep my mind off of things, but I just couldn't. Why would he call me, I hadn't seen him or his wife in my Lamaze class in weeks. Wonder if he told her about me. Doubt it. Anyway, I reached the door to the restaurant; I was about to go in when I heard someone yelling my name. I turned and it was Montel. I wanted to escape but I couldn't, he was on me.

"Hey Sasha, wait a minute. You don't have to ignore me. I was hoping I'd run into you sooner than later."

I rolled my eyes and turned my back as if I didn't see him or hear what he just said.

"Damn, can you at least give me one minute of your time Sasha, please?" He grabbed my arm so I couldn't walk away. "Look, I know things aren't how you wanted and it's my entire fault, but damn we can't even talk to each other? We can't even try to be amicable?"

I looked at him as if he was crazy. "Amicable? You lied to me. You cheated on me. You are married and have a baby on the way. How can I be amicable to that?"

"Jennifer had the baby a couple of weeks ago."

I quickly said, "Congratulations," and tried to go inside.

Once again, he stopped me. "Damn, Sasha, I tried to say the right words but they all just get mixed up. I try to call you, you either aren't there or don't return my calls. I've written you a thousand letters, which I can't seem to send to you in fear that I won't get one back. What can I do to make this up to you? What can I do for us to be friends again? I miss that so much."

"You can't be married. But seeing how that isn't going to happen, I am afraid to say there is nothing you can do, so just go."

"No, I am not leaving until you say yes."

"Say yes to what?"

"That you will try to call me? That you will try to understand my situation? That you will consider holding me in your heart?"

I tried to let my words come out without crying. "I still hold you in my heart. That is the problem."

Montel looked at me and put his hands on my shoulder. "Can I call you sometime?"

"You don't need permission to call me."

"I just want to make sure it's okay with you."

"Call me and say what?"

"I don't know. I'll cross that road when I get to it."

"Whatever, Montel. Look I have to go, I'm meeting someone."

"Who, your new man?"

I wanted to tell him, but didn't because I knew it would lead to another discussion and Michael would come and see me out here with him and things just wouldn't be right. Michael is already asking me too many questions already about Montel.

"Look, just go."

Montel stood there for a few minutes and gave me his look that sent heat waves through me. He kissed me on my forehead, another one displeased with my behavior. Montel walked away, just as he walked out of my life before. I tried not to let his words get in me, but it was too late. He was on me. Still wanted me. Still in my heart. I didn't want to think like that. Here I had Michael who was a wonderful person, a true friend, a true lover, all of the above, and all I could think about was Montel.

I stared down at the scorpion bowl that Michael and I were sipping on; thoughts of Montel ruled my head. I thought about when we first met, when we first kissed, when we made love, how happy he made me. I would give anything to get that feeling back. I was doomed and apparently out of touch with reality. Montel was married; thoughts like this could only lead to trouble.

"Hello Sasha, are you with me or what?"

"Yeah, I'm here. Why, what's up?"

"What's up is you haven't said a word since we got here. You seem distant. Do you think you made the wrong choice about leaving the hospital?"

Poor Michael, so far from what was really going on with me. "No, I'm getting past that; I think I'll be okay. I just have to tell everyone. They won't be too pleased, but it is my life right?"

"You got that right. If they really love you they'll support your decision. Then they have to get over the fact that they will not be able to borrow money from you for a while."

I laughed.

"So, I was thinking, I have this weekend off. Let's go somewhere like Las Vegas for the weekend. You gamble?"

"Oh Montel, I just really don't feel like it." I grabbed my mouth with my hands because I couldn't believe what I just said.

Michael withdrew with disgust in his eyes.

"I am so sorry, Michael. I meant Michael, you've got to know that. There is no Montel."

"Yeah, but you wish there were."

"No I don't."

"Face it, Sasha, you are not over him. How could you be? You never talk about him."

"Hey, I'm trying to get over him, but it takes time, you know that. Look how long it took for you to get over your wife. I was hurt real bad, and I have to move on, I know. But I'm learning how to do that everyday. Hey, we're all right aren't we?"

I stroked his cheek with my hand and smiled. He pulled away.

"Hey, let's get out of here," I suggested with a let's knock boots look.

He pulled away again, as if I repulsed him. "You can't say things like that and put sex on a platter like it solves everything. It doesn't. Sex only makes it worse, harder to let go, harder to get over."

I felt as if he was accusing me of something I didn't do, something I thought about but didn't do. I was about to get on the defensive. "I don't think sex is the answer to everything, and I don't think I like what you are implying."

"What am I implying, that you are sleeping with Montel? That is your guilty conscious working. If you're not sleeping together, then you are thinking about it. If you're not thinking about it, then you probably will be soon anyway, if you don't just let go. Face the fact that he is gone."

Michael's words cut through me like a paper shredder. Bottom line, he was pissing me off. "Look, you don't have to worry about my issues and me, okay? Don't worry your pretty little head about it. See that's why I didn't want a relationship, but you keep pushing and pushing and you just don't seem to understand that these things take time. I can't cut my feelings on and off like the electric company does your lights. I thought you could understand, but you don't. What's the big deal anyway? I haven't committed to any relationship with you. We're just kicking it. If I want to sleep with Montel, I will. You know what your problem is? You are too judgmental. You want everything and everyone to follow your rules and follow your commands. Well I'm sorry that I don't fit in your academy, officer. I'm sorry that I am such a weak link!"

"I think you need to stop there before you make a mistake," Michael warned me.

"Too late for that one!"

I rolled my eyes at Michael and turned my head as if I wasn't even with him.

"Yeah, I think that sums it all up, Ms. Sasha." Michael threw a couple of dollars to cover the tab and looked like he was going to say something like I will call you later but instead he said, "fuck it." He left me there, sitting alone. I kept saying to myself that was bound to happen, we never got along anyway. I'm just glad I didn't waste too much time on him.

On the way home, I tried to go over what was going on in my life. I tried to convince myself that Michael and I didn't belong. We didn't fit together and he would always be judging me and making me seem so incorrect. I then thought about Montel, who never corrected me and only thought the world of me. Only if Montel could be available, like Michael and Michael could be everything but unavailable, like Montel. I don't think I would ever be satisfied until I got my way. I always got half of the broomstick, but not the entire broom.

Here I was twenty-eight years old, no man, no career, and no money. I should be swinging from monkey bars with joy. When I was a kid, I always pictured this happy life at this age. I thought I'd be married, have a few kids, and be successful and loved. Instead I had none of the above. What a crap of shit. You plan your whole life out and nothing is as it should be. I just thank the Lord for my health and my strength to get through all of this disappointment.

I reached my house, and tried to convince myself that things would get better; that I have a purpose, and everything was going to be fine. Dressed in my pajamas, up at 12 a.m. with insomnia, I read a book and tried to shut out all that was in my head, silence it. Then my phone rang. I was sure it was Michael calling to apologize. He was so predictable. I let it ring four times, so he wouldn't think I was up waiting for him to call. I answered the phone and the voice from the earphone was not Michael but Montel.

"It's too late for you to be calling me," I said, really trying to mean it.

"I know, but I had to talk to you again. Look Sasha, I need to see you; there are some things I didn't tell you today, and some things I need you to know. Since you were so busy shoeing me off so you could be with the next man, I didn't get to finish. But I need to talk to you real soon."

I thought *no he did not say I was too busy with the next man. Was he this bold!* "What is real soon, Montel?"

"Like tonight."

"What! What about your wife, what about your baby?"

"My wife and son are at her mother's. She has been staying over there for weeks, to get used to motherhood and all. I'm here all alone."

"I know that is not a signal for me to come over Montel?"

"No, I was just answering your question. Can I come over there?"

"It's late."

"I know, but I just want to talk, you know."

"No. I don't know, Montel. You can't keep doing this, calling me when you need to, running into me when you need to. This has got to stop."

"I know Sash, but I do need you. I will only stay for a little while, please."

I heard the desperation in his voice. I tried to speak another no, but the only word that came out of my mouth was, "Whatever".

I crept downstairs to my house like a burglar, ashamed of who was coming over. I wanted to make sure Raymond was either home or not home. . With a swift look out the window, I saw no car. *Good, No one will see this one.* I kept convincing myself that nothing was going to happen between Montel and me. He was just coming over to talk, nothing else. I said these words as I checked myself out in the mirror. I had on my pajamas, the ones with the skintight tank top and little booty shorts. Those were my favorite, Montel's too. He said I looked so cute in them. *Oh, here I go. No damn it, the man is married, he has a child. I am no home wrecker. He's just coming over to finish things up with us.*

After saying those words to myself, I wasn't so sure I was ready to finish things up with us. *Damn it, why does it have to be this way,* I kept saying to myself. *Why is love so damn complicated? If two people are in love then they should be together.* Things should be as simple as that. I didn't want to hurt anyone, I would hate for someone to break up my marriage. But what was their marriage based on? It couldn't have been that strong, if he was calling me up this late. I was starting to sound like

Tammy. I never want to do that to anyone, what Tammy was doing to Michelle's marriage. I just had to be strong.

I got to thinking about T and Ricky. They were in love. They were together. T just said later for the wife! Why couldn't I do that? Why was I reading into this so much? Whatever, I don't know why I am beating myself up about this. I hadn't made any calls; I hadn't arranged any secret rendezvous. Montel was the one in control; I was just an innocent bystander, trying to figure out where I fit in all of this. After minutes of pondering, I came to the conclusion that what ever happened was not my fault. I didn't ask for any of this. I still loved Montel and if we were meant to be together, then like Michelle said, we would.

After waiting fifty minutes for Montel to arrive, I could hear Tasha upstairs, walking back and forth. Raymond wasn't home yet; she must have been waiting up for him. My house was so silent and still I could hear everything. The phone upstairs rang. Tasha answered on the first ring, as if she was waiting for the call. She answered a loud "Hello". Whoever was on the phone with her, she didn't sound to pleased with them.

"Why did I page you, nigger? I paged you cause I needed to talk to you. I have been hearing some stupid shit, you running your mouth about business that isn't yours. You keep talking and you will see what happens to you… What! Test me nigga, and see what happens. Look, you need to keep all that nonsense to yourself. I'm doing what is best for me, not you, for me. You didn't want anything to do with me, so now you hear I'm doing good without you and you want a piece of this pie. It's too late; I have moved on. I'm getting married. You heard about that, huh? What? Yeah I am pregnant, so? Nigga, fuck you, I know who my baby's father is! No it isn't you, and if you keep spreading that bullshit, I'm going to put one in you, ya heard! Whatever nigga, yeah see me around!"

Tasha slammed the phone so hard I could hear it all the way downstairs. What was that all about? I never heard Tasha talk in such language; it was like she was a different person. Ghetto fabulous or something. This was not the sweet, innocent girl I had come to know. What was really going on? She must have been talking to some dude, some no-name cat. And what was this about her getting married? Raymond hadn't set any date. Not by my watch anyway. I'd been putting this off too long; I needed to find out what was really going on real soon. Tasha was up to something, and I was going to be the one to find out what.

The time was now 2 a.m. It shouldn't have taken Montel that long to come over. As I made my way upstairs, I heard a car pulling up in my driveway. I was certain it was Raymond, and I did want to talk to him about Tasha anyway, so I went to the door. Well, if it wasn't Mr. Hayes. About time. Montel ran up the stairs and quickly into my house to fight the rainy weather. He kissed my cheek, "Did I take too long?"

"Yeah, you did. I was just about to go to bed."

"Oh, well I don't want to hold you up from getting any sleep."

"So, what did you have to discuss with me in person that you couldn't say to me over the phone?"

"Can I take my coat off, get a little comfy first before I begin this?"

"No, cause I doubt you'll be here that long. You can have a seat over there."

"Your place looks nice, Sasha. It smells good in here. I remember when you used to dedicate Saturdays to your clean up days. No other day of the week was appropriate."

"I never had time during the week, but now I have all the time in the world."

"I see, you teaching Lamaze and working at the hospital."

"No Montel, FYI, I don't work at the hospital anymore, I quit."

"What? I thought your work meant a lot to you. You were always there, you spent more time there than with me."

"What? Montel you were the one who was always off, somewhere, promoting this group and that group, in another city or state."

"I made time for you, though."

"Obviously not enough time, since you went off and got some other girl pregnant and then married her. What's up with that? Oh now you're all silent, as if that didn't happen. You make me sick."

"Do I really? I don't mean to, you have to know that. What I felt for you, no what I still feel for you is right here. This isn't going anywhere; that is what I came to tell you. This is why I had to see you to tell you this. I don't know how long I can live this lie with Jennifer, but I want you to know that you are the only woman for me. I don't care how long it is going to take or who you are with at the time. I am going to make you mine some day. It may not be today, but I will. Trust me."

"Trust you, Montel? How can I trust you? Look at what you've done to us; look at the mess you've made. If I'm the only woman for you, how come you weren't thinking about that when you and Jennifer were one night standing it? Look at you. Can you honestly look me in the face and say it was only one time, that the whole time me and you were together, it was always about us? Not her, not anyone?"

"Yes!" Montel answered me. "Listen, Sasha, I told you what happened between Jennifer and I was just one night, just one moment. I was weak. I let her in. I should have been trying to figure out what went wrong with us. I know you can't understand it now, but I'm begging you to please try to understand. When she told me she was pregnant, I felt like I had no choice but to marry her."

"Yeah, yeah, cause you grew up without a father. But you still could have been a father; you didn't have to be married to do that."

"Yes I did. I felt I did."

"And now how do you feel?"

"I feel like I am going to fuck everyone's life up, yours, hers, my son's life and mine. I thought I was doing what needed to be done, but now I see what a mistake I made."

"How long before the wedding did you decide to marry her after she told you she was pregnant?"

"About a month."

"So in one month's time, you still didn't feel the need to tell me? I had to find out the way I did? When did you plan on telling me?"

"The bachelor's party was a surprise, I didn't know about that. I had plans on telling you before the wedding, I just didn't know what I was going to say."

"I see."

"How did you find out about the party anyway?"

"Detective Perry came across it on his way to my birthday party."

"Oh my number one fan huh? I bet he's been around more now huh?"

"I thought you were here to talk about us?"

"I know, just the thought of you with another man, you just don't know what it does to me."

"How do you think I feel? I had to sit there while you and your wife played house. Do you have any idea how unimportant that made me feel?"

"I know, but look, I'm trying to do right by you, and I just need you to stop shutting me out. You said I make you sick, give me the chance to make you feel better that's all I ask."

I wanted to give him that chance. I needed to know what was going to become of us in order for me to truly move on. "Look Montel, I don't know. I can't be sneaking around with you like that, and I wouldn't feel right."

"What, you think this is about sex? Come on, Sasha, you know better. I'm trying to stay in your life that's all. Will you give me that chance?"

Montel started his stares at me; those chinky eyes were the ones that heated me up. Damn, I loved this man so much, how could I let him go so easy. I tried not to seem weak or show that he had won.

"Can I call you later?" Montel asked.

"I just can't answer that right now. I need to work some things out on my own, see what I want to do."

"I understand, Sash, just don't forget about me. I won't let you."

I gave him a soft hug that seemed to last forever. How could I let him back in my life? "If I do decide to let you back in my life, it will be just as friends, that is it. You're married and I'm not about to break up a happy home, ya heard."

"I feel you. I'll take whatever I can get from you. I need you in my life, Sasha, and that is for real."

With those last words, I fell asleep on the couch with Montel. I didn't want to send him out in the rain, it was late, too, and he could bunk here for the night. I fell asleep with such fear that we could never be like this again, that our innocent love was about to turn into something ugly. I kept saying to myself, "friends" that's all I needed from him. I was lying to myself, because I knew that I would always want more. I would always want him to myself. I didn't know what was going to happen, just that I needed him in my life as much as he needed me. So there we slept with no easy road to take, no easy way to love each other without hurting someone. We still slept though, with the understanding that one day we would be together.

CHAPTER TWENTY

"Sasha, what do you think of this table?"

Lisa wanted my expert advice on redecorating her place. I don't know why she brought me all the way down here at 8 in the morning to go furniture shopping. Her place was fine. I guess she wanted something different.

"Lisa, everything you have shown me is nice. Why are you redecorating your house? Christmas is like in two weeks, do you honestly think this is the time for redecorations?"

"Yeah girl, there's no time like the present. Besides, I've gotten all of Jasmine's toys and everyone else's presents, so I thought I'd fix up the place."

"Okay, fix up the place, not buy an entire room or two."

"Do you think it's too much?" Lisa asked me with uncertainty.

"Well, look at this bedroom set you've picked out. It doesn't look too dainty for a woman's bedroom set. And what about this table? It looks more neutral, masculine even. You're a single mom with a child. This doesn't look like single mom and one child furniture. You're picking out family, Mom and Dad and children furniture."

"It's that obvious, huh?" Lisa smiled.

What was this girl talking about? I had my own issues to deal with. I still didn't know what I was going to do about my career. I still hadn't figured out what Tasha was up to, and I didn't know what the hell Montel and I were doing.

Since the night we talked, that fool had been calling me everyday. We met everyday this week for lunch. When did he spend time with his wife? This so-called friendship had gone on for like a month now. Not to mention the fact that I was still stringing Michael along. He called me the next day after our fight. We talked and both agreed to take things slow, not rush each other, whatever that meant.

I had already made up my mind that Montel and I would be together. Jennifer and Michael were just little obstacles that we had to bypass in time. This so-called friendship got a little deeper here and there. Last week when Montel came by late, a night I had to make sure Michael was working, we almost slept together. If it weren't for Tasha's false labor interruption, we probably would have.

Tasha had a couple of false alarms, all this month. Every night, I'd think it's time. That's all that comes out of her mouth, besides questions about marriage. My question was when and if Raymond was going to marry this girl? If he was, it didn't look like he was in any rush. I barely saw Raymond. He worked at the fire station late, and his second job, construction, was early in the morning. That boy must have been saving a fortune. As long as he kept up his payment for the rent, I wasn't too concerned.

Then again, when was I ever around? Between Michael and Montel, it seemed like I had been working two jobs. Oh well, I tried to avoid Montel but he was always in my face, always making it seem like we were meant to be together. I tried to make him focus on his wife and son, but when he was with me, it was like he was in another world. I couldn't call it. I was trying to keep things on the friendly tip, so I couldn't be blamed for whatever happened. Michael pretended to be clueless about my feelings for Montel. He protected himself that way. Oh everything was such a mess. Anyway, I kept telling myself that I was not responsible. And as long as Michael played along I would play with him and as long as Montel was married, him and I were just going to be friends. That's right. No sex, no kissing, no nothing; no matter how I felt about him.

As Lisa rambled on to the next table, she looked at me for approval. I nodded like I nodded at all the other tables. She was really starting to bug me. I had to meet Michael to help him pick out a present for his mother. I made plans to meet with Ray to discuss Tasha finally, and I still hadn't finished my Christmas shopping. Lisa needed to come on. After we reached the last set of tables, I snapped. "Lisa you have dragged me through this entire store. We have looked at every table in here and you still haven't picked one out yet. Would you come on, I have some things to do today."

Lisa looked at me, like whatever she had to tell me was very important.

"What girl, what's up?" I said.

"Okay, I didn't bring you down here to help me shop. I brought you down here because I needed to tell you something. I figured that if I kind of hinted at what was going on with Damon and me, you would guess. But seeing how you're clueless, I'll just tell you. Damon and I are moving in together." She took one breath and put her hand on top of mine as if she were bracing me.

I said, "How nice for you and Damon."

I didn't see the point of Lisa trying to be subtle about this. So you and Damon are moving in together, woopty doo! I have my own issues. That's what I felt like saying to Lisa, but I remained happy for her. "You know Lisa that is really good. So things are moving along then. Does this mean this time next year I'll have a wedding to go to?"

"I don't know. We're just going to try this moving in together first, see how things work out. Then who knows, anything is possible." Lisa smiled.

"My thoughts exactly," I replied.

"I just wanted to make sure things were okay with us first before I told everyone else."

"Lisa you do not need my stamp of approval when it comes to you and Damon. I'm over him and I don't even look at him the same. You two are together and he makes you happy, that's all that matters with me. Do your thang, Ma."

Lisa smiled. Those words I said, I meant. I was never in love with Damon, and I was definitely not holding any feelings for him. Granted I didn't like the idea of him dating one of my girls, but by the time I found out, it was too late. Lisa had fallen for him. Who was I to interfere with that? As Michelle said things happen for a reason.

I finally left the store with Lisa. Then I met up with Michael to pick up a few things for his mother and my laundry list of presents I had to buy. We went to the South Mall. Of course it was packed, nothing good left on the racks. Everything was sold out. Yet, we tried to find some items. Once we reached Macy's it was like a mob house. I suggested to Michael he buy his mother an expensive scarf or some perfume. He couldn't go wrong with that. I made my way to the jewelry counter.

Aunt Mimi, Tanya, and I made it a point to buy each other jewelry each Christmas. I just wondered what I was going to get. I hope it was that gold bangle I had my eye on. Anyway, I picked up a pretty set of gold earrings for Tanya and a bracelet for Aunt Mimi. Two items I would love to see on myself. Just then, I found myself staring at the diamond engagement rings.

I let my fantasy run wild. I pictured Montel and I during Christmas, shopping together. I would be eyeing platinum diamond rings and he would pretend not to see me staring at it. On Christmas day he would surprise me with it and ask me to marry him. Oh, I smiled at the thought. Wouldn't that just be grand! The sales woman, who asked me did I need anything, interrupted my fantasy. I reluctantly declined and made my way back to find Michael. I passed the scarf section, no Michael. I figured he must have made his way to the men's section and started shopping for himself. Michael and I were alike in that way. We tried to do for other people, but never forgot about ourselves. He was probably in the shoe section. Michael loved his shoes. As I passed the jackets and trousers I found the shoe section and sure enough, he was there. I crept up on him while he was at the register and put my hands in his pocket.

"Hey Santa, this doesn't look like the scarf section," I whispered in his ear.

Michael turned around and gave me a kiss on my lips.

"What are you buying Santa?" I asked.

"Just a little bit of this and a little bit of that," he replied.

"Anything in the bag for Mrs. Claus?"

"Yeah I bought my mother a nice scarf."

"I was referring to myself!"

Michael knew that, but he liked to pretend he didn't. Another way he protected his feelings. Michael gave me a kiss on my forehead and put his arm around me. I was trying to walk in my direction when he was persuading me to go the other way, as if he knew something I didn't. Just as we played tug of war to try to get to the other side, I saw why Michael wanted me to go his way instead of mine. Montel was shopping for shoes as well, not alone. Of course, he was with his wife and baby. I tried to glance away before he saw me, but it was too late. He saw me, and his wife's eyes were not too far behind him. I didn't know if I should wave or just pretend I didn't know them. I was hoping she had a bad memory but I was wrong. As I passed, she said, "Hey, didn't you teach Lamaze class at the YMCA?"

I replied, "Yeah, isn't your name, Janet?"

"Jennifer. You remember my husband Montel?" Jennifer gestured her hand toward Montel.

I said my hello, as if I didn't know this man. Still playing along, "Well I see you had your baby. Labor wasn't too hard for you, was it?"

"No, one day of your class really helped. I still had an epidural, but the pain wasn't that bad. I recommended a few friends to your class. They should be calling you."

Great! Why did she have to be so damn nice! "Well it was nice seeing you again. Congratulations, you have yourself a beautiful baby."

Jennifer smiled and said thank you. I gave Montel the stares that said all I was feeling inside. I couldn't have walked out of Macy's fast enough. Michael was trailing behind me, not saying a word. All that went through my head was how could I be so cold, so nonchalant. That just tore me up inside. I saw the man that I wanted to marry with his wife and child, and I pretended like I didn't even know him. I knew this wouldn't work. I knew I couldn't just remain neutral, go on with my life as if I didn't want to have any part of his. By the time we reached the car my brain was fried. I was not in the mood for small talk or interrogation by Michael, but of course he didn't understand that. H*ere we go*.

"I see you still are holding a candle for that one, huh?" Michael asked.

"I knew you weren't going to let this opportunity go by."

"All I am saying is, I could see what was going on back there. The tension between you two was obvious."

"What tension?"

"As if something is going on with you two."

You know Michael's insecurities really pissed me off. It wasn't that he was right. What pissed me off was that I couldn't fool him. Every chance he got he would drill me about Montel. When was the last time you spoke? if he wasn't married would you still be with him, and blah, blah? He would go on and on, like he was trying to get me to confess. It just made me so very mad. "Michael, for the umpteenth time there is nothing going on between

Montel and me. We are friends." *Oops, how did that slip out? Last I told Michael, Montel and I didn't even speak*, I thought.

"Friends since when?" Michael said with a confused look on his face.

"Since I don't know, since I met him." I was trying to get out of that one, but I couldn't. I had spilled the beans.

"Sasha, is there something you'd like to tell me?"

"Michael, we are all right, right?"

"I used to think so until lately. I feel you're distant from me, or holding back on me because you're waiting for someone else to come along."

"I like us Michael, I do. I just, I don't know! Everything seemed to move so fast when we said it would move slowly. I haven't had a chance to figure everything out."

"You mean you haven't had a chance to realize that I am the one for you, not Montel?"

What, where did that come from? I thought. If Michael knew this whole time that I still was in love with Montel; why did he even bother with me? Why go through the pain and disappointment?

"Michael, you don't understand."

"I understand more than you know. But I'm not going to sit around and watch you make an ass out of me and an ass out of yourself. You and Montel have some unfinished business and we can't move forward unless you face that."

What? Was Michael testing me to see if I would fall for that one? "Montel is married. There is no business between us, we are over."

"I wish that was true, Sasha. I wish that was true."

Michael didn't say much to me on the way to my house. He dropped me off, thanked me for helping him find something for his mother, and drove off. I couldn't understand it. In one way, I thought he was testing me to see what I would do if I had the chance to be with Montel. On the other hand, I thought he was trying to flip it on me by pretending he didn't care, so I wouldn't think his feelings were into this. Michael shouldn't play so many mind games. He should just say what he felt.

Anyways, I dropped off my shopping bags and met Ray for lunch to warn him about Tasha and to see what was going on with this marriage thing. I met him downtown at this place my mother used to take us called Aunt Bernie's Grill. I couldn't wait to eat.

"Hey, sis! I haven't seen you in a minute. Michael keeping you busy?"

I looked at Raymond like, how do you know anything is going on with Michael and me? I thought I was playing this friendship role pretty good.

"Big Sis, don't front. I know the brother has got a thing for you, and you got something for him too."

"Look Ray, big Sis can handle hers. I want to talk to you about Tasha. What's up, you two getting married?"

Raymond looked at me like, don't go there please.

"She's about to set a date if you don't say anything Ray, what's up? She's about drop that load any day now, so if you plan on marrying her, I suggest you do so soon."

"I know. That's why I have been working both these jobs." Raymond smiled and pulled out a black box. Inside the box was a gold band with a 1-carat Marquise diamond inside.

"Oh Raymond, you two really are getting married. I thought this was all in her head?"

"At first, I wanted to see how things were going to go with us. I met Tasha after I broke up with Tina. In a week we slept together. In six weeks she tells me she is pregnant, so I wasn't really sure about her. But in all this time we've spent together, she has grown on me, and I'm ready to make that step. We share the same space and now we're about to share a life. For real, Tasha is the one, and I didn't even know it. I was messing with this chick and that one for a minute. But ever since Tasha came along and put it on me, all I want is her."

It was funny to hear Raymond talk about his Tasha this way. Love was truly in the air. I was happy for Raymond, but cautious for him too for I knew what love brought. "Wow, you're only twenty-three. How do you know what love is?"

"Hey, this is what I feel love is. Therefore this is what it is going to be. Me, Tasha, and the baby forever."

"I see. Well, when did you meet her in like February, pregnant in April, due in December?"

"I know where you're going, Sasha. Don't. I thought you liked Tasha?"

"I did, but something is off about her. Like I heard her on the phone talking to some dude."

"Some dude, when?"

"Like a month ago, at least I thought it was a dude. She said something like she has moved on, getting married, having a baby, no not yours. I don't know. I am not trying to place doubt in your head, but something doesn't seem right."

"Sasha, I'm a grown man. Let me worry about Tasha. If she's playing me for a fool, she will feel it. That seed she is carrying is my seed and I don't want to hear anything more about it."

"Fine. I just wanted to give you a heads up. I've got to look out for my brother."

"Yeah, well don't worry."

That love-sick look in Ray's eyes let me know how snowed he was on Tasha. It never dawned on him that she would be lying about her pregnancy. Why would she? I don't know. For her sake I hoped she was telling the truth, because Ray's temper was unpredictable. I couldn't go through another court case, which is why I wanted to prepare him for the upset.

"Well Raymond, I trust you can handle your business. I just want to remind you that women take care of women in their own way. Just like men take care of men, in theirs."

"Enough, Sasha, I got this."

I backed off.

"I know how scandalous woman can be, Sasha."

"Men can be just as scandalous."

"Yeah, well um what up with Montel? Tasha told me she saw him coming out of your place the other night."

I almost choked on my water. "What?"

Raymond laughed, "No need to deny it, big Sis. I see your game. You're playing Michael close, but you got yourself a spare if you need it."

More like the other way around. Michael was the spare. I nodded like that's what was really going on.

"You don' t have to explain, you know what you are doing." Raymond responded.

How could Ray be so sure that I did?

"See you haven't reached that level yet with someone special, someone you can trust. Because if you did, you wouldn't need a spare, ya heard."

That's what I thought I was doing with Montel. I didn't think I needed a spare when we were together. I also thought I could trust him. Boy was I wrong. "Yeah, Raymond, I know what I'm doing. Let's just leave it at that."

"Say no more, Sasha." Raymond paid for lunch and went on about his merry little way.

All day I thought about Montel. How easy Lisa had found trust in Damon, how easy Raymond found trust in Tasha. Why wasn't it so easy for me? T and Ricky even hooked back up, how crazy was that? Michelle still clung on to Jamal. After all his dirt, she was still with him. Tanya and Larry kept it going strong for years. What was my problem? As I let my thoughts take over, my phone rang. It was Montel. It was late of course, twelve in the morning, his regular time for calling.

"Hey baby girl, what's up?"

"Nothing, just sitting here thinking."

"You want some company?"

I thought *yeah but not you.* "Montel, I think I need some distance between us."

"What? Why?" He sounded confused.

"Because you're making me crazy. You are married. We can toy along with the idea that we are just friends, but you and I both know the real deal. I can't live like this."

"Oh, what you and my man getting serious or something?"

Montel was always directing the attention from himself. "No, Montel. I just don't think you are giving your marriage a try, if you're always calling me."

"You're not making sense. You know what my marriage is based on. You know who I wanted to marry, you. So why are you trying to flip the script on me?"

"Because you are married, and it isn't to me. The longer I hold on to you the harder it is for me to let go."

"I thought you didn't want to let go?"

"I didn't, but things are so complicated. I try to be friends with you, but when we're alone, I can't help my feelings. One of these days things are going to get out of control. Then where will we end up? A lot of people are going to get hurt if we keep carrying on this way Montel."

"So what are you saying? You don't want to be with me?"

I paused, trying to get my words right, trying to make it come out right. "I can't be with you, is what I am saying, Montel. I can't."

Montel was silent for a long time. I had to say hello to make sure he was still there.

"Yeah all right Ms. Sasha, I'll see you around." Montel hung up.

I tried to sleep, but couldn't. I don't know what just came over me. How could I end things with Montel when I swore we'd be together. Maybe it was my subconscious trying to flip the script on Montel, like Michael was trying to do to me. Make it seem like I didn't want him, so he would want me. In the middle of my thoughts, the doorbell rang. To no surprise it was Montel.

"What are you doing here?" I asked.

Montel said nothing. He busted in and kissed me hard. He started to undo my robe but I stopped him.

"Montel, I can't. What about your wife?"

Montel looked at me. "What about us? You don't know how much I wish things were different. You don't know how much I want to be with you. Every day I wake up to her, and I wish it were you I was holding. Sasha, you know why I'm here. I am not letting you go. You can't let me go, you know that." Montel began to kiss me. He had a crazy look in his face. He was determined to break me, to make me see things his way. I tried to fight, Lord knows I did. He began to undress me. He slid his fingers in me.

I moaned as I tried to pull away. "Montel, this is wrong."

He silenced me with his kisses. He tongued me down. I tried to fight him some more. My defenses were becoming weary.

"Montel, do you love me?"

"If you don't know the answer to that, why are we here? This isn't lust I feel, this is love. I can't breathe without you. I can't think without you. Don't turn me loose please," Montel begged. He kissed me again, undid his clothes, undid my clothes, and slid inside me. A half an hour later, the deed was done. The line was crossed. There was no turning back.

The doorbell rang, then the knocking started. The knock was crazy, like the police were at the door. I tried to get up but I couldn't. Something was wearing me down, I couldn't move. The knock got louder and louder. I heard footsteps. I tried to get up, I had this sick feeling in my stomach, and I felt terrified. I tried to find out what was holding me down, so heavy, that I couldn't get up. The footsteps got louder and louder, my door to my bedroom opened. The shadow from this figure was dark, so dark I couldn't see the person's face. The doorbell was still ringing, someone was yelling. Sasha, Sasha, you better get out of there. I tried to get up, I tried to move, and I still couldn't. I realized that a body was holding me down, Montel's body. He was dead. I looked up as a woman with a knife stood over me. There was blood dripping from the knife. I screamed, I kicked, I still couldn't move. The face came clear. It was Tammy.

I woke up, to the knocking on my door. Sweat poured from my forehead. It was 3 in the morning.

"Sash's she's going to have the baby," Raymond yelled.

I could hear Raymond yelling through my door. I rushed out of bed. I could hear the sirens from the ambulance.

"Sasha, she doesn't look too good, she's bleeding. I called the ambulance and Tasha said she can't breathe."

I rushed down stairs and threw my robe on. I was naked underneath from doing the deed. I opened the door. "Where is she, Raymond, where is she?"

"Upstairs."

Raymond pulled my arm and dragged me upstairs.

I yelled, "Tasha, honey, breathe. You have to breathe."

Tasha was turning blue, she needed oxygen, and she was hyperventilating. I found an empty Burger King bag on the floor and told her to breathe through it.

"How long has she been like this? Have you been counting the contractions?"

"Yeah, they're like seven, maybe eight minutes apart!" Raymond shouted.

She looked very puffy in the face, her ankles were swollen.

"Okay. Looks like she has eclampsia."

"Eclampsia who?" Raymond questioned.

"High blood pressure. It isn't good for her or the baby. Tasha, I need you to keep breathing slowly into this bag. I can hear the ambulance, you're going to be okay."

A squad car got to my house before the ambulance. I ran into my house to put on some clothes to go with Raymond and Tasha to the hospital.

"Sasha, are you alright?" A frantic Michael came through the door.

I was surprised and terrified all at the same time. "Yeah, it is okay, Tasha's in labor."

I tried to steer Michael away from the bedroom, so he couldn't see who was lying in the bed. I wasn't fast enough. Michael could see the trail of men's clothes on the floor, leading to Montel's yellow back. Michael didn't say a word. He just looked at me with such contempt, like he wished he didn't even know me. I couldn't say a word. I was ashamed. I wanted to say, well you said I had unfinished business with him. But I knew that wasn't the right thing to say.

Raymond yelled for me, "She's getting worse, Sasha."

I grabbed my medical bag and ran to Tasha. I took her blood pressure. It was 200/100, too high. She definitely was eclamptic. The ambulance came. I explained the situation and they proceeded to start I.V. fluids running and oxygen.

I tried to reassure Raymond that everything was going to be okay. "Just stay with her, Raymond, I'm right behind you." The ambulance door closed. I turned and Michael was still there. He looked at me, but said nothing. I didn't say anything either. What could I say? Michael now saw all of me, even my darkest side, and my unprettiness.

"I have to follow the ambulance," I said in a monotone voice.

"You have to do what you have to do."

I grabbed my keys inside my house. Montel was up and at the door. He asked me was everything all right and did I need him to go to the hospital with me.

Michael then interrupted and said, "Don't you have a wife, no excuse me, a family to go home to?"

Montel looked at Michael, Michael looked at Montel. No words, just eye contact. They were nose-to-nose, chest-to-chest, standing off. I looked at both of them. One who brought me so much joy and at the same time, so much pain. The other who only wanted to make me happy, and protect me from harm, even if that harm was self inflicted. I couldn't choose sides. I feared neither side was right at that time. Montel and Michael walked around each other still saying nothing. Montel, who was now on the outside of the door, backed off and left Michael standing beside me. He smiled as he said, "Call me later, Sash, and let me know if everything is all right."

Michael said with fire in his voice like a dragon, "Good night," as he waved goodbye to Montel.

Michael turned to me and still said nothing. I eased by him and locked the door. I tried to walk away before he got the chance to say anything to me, before I could hear the hatred in his voice. Like always, Michael started at me. "So this is what you want? Him? It has always been him?"

I turned to Michael, crying. "Michael, I don't know what I want. Can't you see I'm torn, I am confused right now?"

"Ms. Freeman, you don't want to know what I see."

That was all that needed to be said. I turned and got into my car and drove off. I stopped crying on the way to the hospital. I erased whatever guilt I felt, whatever wrongs I felt. I kept saying to myself, it isn't my fault. It isn't my fault.

By the time I got to the hospital, Tasha was on the operating table. I found Raymond hunched over with his hands buried in his face. I sat next to him, and laid my head on his shoulder. Raymond began to cry. "She has got to make it, she has to." We sat in the waiting room for an hour. The doctor came out and congratulated Raymond on a healthy baby boy. Raymond jumped up and said, "What about Tasha?"

The doctor smiled and said everything is all right. "Is this your sister?"

"Yeah, this is lil Ray's auntie, Sasha."

I wiped my tears of joy and said to Raymond, "You already have a name for him?"

The doctor patted me on the back and said, "They wouldn't have made it without your fast thinking. Are you a doctor?"

"Well, I was. It's a long story. I am just glad to see everything is all right. Thank you, Dr…?"

"Dr. Walters. If you're not in medicine, you need to get back in it real soon. We need strong-headed doctors like yourself in the field working."

I took that in, but I still didn't appreciate any compliments. I was dirt as of right now. Raymond, Tasha, and little Raymond were doing fine. I went home to get their things. Tasha had to stay in the hospital a couple of days. I had a few messages on my phone. The most important one was from T, telling me that Michelle had gone into labor and delivered a girl. I had to sit down. All this in one night. It was too much for me to grasp. On my way back to the hospital, I stopped by Boston General where Michelle had delivered, to check out this new edition to her family. Lisa and T were already there, arguing over who would be the Godmother.

"Damn, can I know the little one's name first?" I busted in.

"Sasha, where have you been?" Lisa demanded.

"Long story, didn't come here to talk about me. Let me hold my new Godchild."

I made the googoos and gagas at the precious little thing.

"Michelle, honey you looked worn out. Where is Jamal?" I asked.

"Probably with his girlfriend."

Silence entered the room.

"Excuse me, his what?" I said.

Michelle took a breath. "I was due two weeks from now, but that asshole made me go into labor."

"What happened?" I questioned.

"You want to know what happened. Christmas is only about ten days away, but Jamal decides he needs a break from all this and will be staying at his brother's house. I say fine, I don't need this shit right now either. So, I bring his stuff over to his brother Tony's house. Marijuana smoke filled the air. I asked where Jamal was. Tony shrugged his shoulders, high as a kite. I go downstairs to the basement and start yelling for Jamal. 'Michelle don't come in here, don't turn on that light,' he starts saying. I go inside, turn on the light, and find my husband and this white woman in bed together."

Our mouths dropped.

"What happened?" I asked Michelle.

"The bitch had the nerve to cover her face with the covers, as if I didn't see her."

T started laughing, "Damn that is messed up."

"So, I calmly say to Jamal, 'I got your stuff upstairs, you can come get the rest tomorrow. Oh and by the way, you under the covers, I hope you wore protection because Jamal has HIV'. The tramp jumped out of the bed and Jamal covered his face like I know she didn't just do that. The girl started screaming and crying and began to attack my husband. I couldn't go for that, so I snatched her up and threw her to the floor. I kicked her ass."

We started laughing.

"And do you know who that hoe was." Michelle continued.

"Who?" Lisa egged on.

"Tammy, the blackmail bitch."

I covered my mouth, to act surprised. "Damn, well that is just one of his hoes."

T said, "Chelle why are you even with this fool?"

"Lord only knows, T, Lord only knows."

"Michelle, you know what you need to do," T said.

"I know, but I feel like who else is going to want me?"

I said, "My Aunt Mimi told me you don't know what is in front of you until you open your eyes, and Michelle you have had your blinders on for years."

"I know," Michelle said.

"Well if you know, then why can't you dig your head out of the snow and stop this madness." I asked her.

"I will some day, ladies, I will. I just don't know when."

"How about now?" T interrupted.

Michelle took a hard look in the mirror, a real good look, like she never saw herself before. "I always thought death do us part, but do I really want to die like this?"

"Only you know the answer to that, Michelle. You think you'll lose something, when you're the one who will be found," I said.

We hugged for a little bit. Lisa told everyone about Damon and her moving in together. I told them about Raymond and Tasha.

I also told them about my drama. Raised eyebrows, but no surprised looks came across their faces. We had all been there, either at the same time or one by one, going back to the ones we should have left behind.

T began to tell us about her drama. "Ricky's wife is trying to hold on, she still hasn't signed the divorce papers."

Lisa interrupted, "That is if Ricky even filed them."

A bunch of hmms and grunts took over the room.

"Don't go there with me," T demanded respect. "I will be the first to admit that I didn't think things would go this way with Ricky and I, but hey, love is something you can't help. Now Ricky and her are through. He realized he made a mistake and it's time to correct it."

"How can you be this forward about it? T, you are sleeping with someone else's husband!" Michelle interjected. "Do I have to remind you of the damage you have done? Look at Jamal and me. You want to be that self-serving bitch!"

"Too late for that,." I added that one in.

T put her hands on her hip and began to break it down for us as to why Ricky and her were the right thing. "Look, first off, Ricky got with her when he was supposed to be marrying me. She was a rebound. She had no business with him in the first place. After years of living with this woman, he realized where he went wrong and who he should be with. Me. We've had a dozen conversations about this. Ricky knows what I want from him, and he's prepared to give it to me. I'm giving him a second chance, and so far, things have worked out. He lives in my suite at the hotel. His wife lives in an apartment on Beacon Street. They don't even share the same space anymore. If you really look at it, I'm doing Ricky's wife a favor. She would have set herself up for a lifetime of pain and disappointment by staying married to him. I'm the woman for him, not her, and he has made that painfully obvious to her."

"How has he made that obvious, T?" I asked.

"For one, he doesn't live there. Two, he spends all his time with me. Three, when he does go by their house to pick things up, I'm either with him, or I call him to make sure he's on his way to my place."

"So she knows about you?" Lisa asked

"Trust me, she knows. If she doesn't shame on her."

"Well, I guess you've made up your mind. Are you making plans for a wedding again?" I asked.

"Hell no!" T said with certainty. "I've come to realize that marriage isn't a part of me. I was just trying to follow along with every other normal couple. The truth is, we can be together and love each other without some marriage certificate."

"I see, so you two are going to be together forever, with no bands?" Michelle questioned.

"Look, I don't need a ceremony to validate our relationship. We love each other and we know how to make it work with us."

"I see. Well I guess your only obstacle is the divorce then," I said.

"Happily ever after, huh?" Lisa added.

"Yeah, just don't marry him, and you two will be fine." Michelle added with a sarcastic twist.

T's attitude shifted, "See that's why I can't tell you anything, Michelle. The way I live my life has nothing to do with Jamal and you. Frankly, Jamal and Ricky are two different people with two different circumstances."

"How so? Ricky dogged you out while y'all were dating. You even admitted that you knew he saw other women." Michelle said.

"Okay, we were like what, eighteen, nineteen?" T said, defensively.

"No, T. You said you knew the type of man Ricky was and you were happy with him as long as that shit didn't creep up on your front door," I added.

"I said that?" T questioned herself. "Well, that was then, this is now. Ricky and I are older, more mature, and know what we want from each other."

T tried to convince us, but she couldn't win. I had my own opinions and issues with Ricky and T's relationship. In my opinion, T was fooling herself trying to make Ricky seem like something he wasn't. He was a dog, just like Jamal. True, Ricky did hook up with his wife during the course of their relationship downs, but he was seeing T now, even though he still was married. I couldn't criticize under similar circumstances. I was sleeping with someone else's husband too. However, no one in this room could tell me that Jamal wasn't a dog and no good. Michelle couldn't ever convince me of that. I wish she would come to her senses on that one.

I said, "Well look, T's mind is made up, so nothing we say or do will convince her otherwise. My question to you T is what do you think about my situation with Montel?"

"Honestly honey, I think you should have left him alone a very long time ago. You are messing up. I understand that he's married and is in that situation because of a child. I know you think if there were no baby, you and he would still be together. The fact of the matter is, Montel has never been persuaded to do anything. He looks out for himself. I still don't think he married her because of a baby. There's more to that story than what he's telling. If he's trying to be such the family man, then why, every chance he gets is he knocking down your front door? As for Michael, he's a decent brother, but if you're not feeling him, you just aren't feeling him. Don't waste your time on him, like I did Linc. In the end, someone gets hurt, and you end up feeling worse."

I took T's advice in my head. I still was going to make my own decision, but I needed another's point of view. I didn't know how I felt about Michael. He had always been there for me, and would do anything for me. I messed up with him that was for sure. I didn't know why, though. I always complain about men being dogs and there are no good men around. The first real man I get, I treat him so bad. Maybe I just didn't deserve a good man. I got what I dished out. Anyways, I cut my thoughts off and changed the subject.

"So Michelle, what are you going to name this little one? Sasha maybe?"

Michelle laughed. "The doctors told me that her HIV test came back negative."

A shout of glee bounced out of our voices.

"I'm so happy and thankful that my weakness and lack of sense for staying with Jamal hasn't affected my children. This little one represents hope that everything is going to be okay. Yeah, Hope. That will be her name. Hope Janeya."

We each held Hope in our hands and made silly faces. I was so happy that things turned out good for Michelle and the baby. I just hoped that our conversation had given her the strength to let that low life Jamal go.

Back at home, I gathered my thoughts and tried to get my life together. I made a list of all the goals I had for the New Year. First on my list was to find a job or career, whichever came first. I hadn't decided what I wanted to do. When Tasha went into labor like that, everything came back to me like riding a bike. I still didn't have a passion for that kind of work. I still didn't have that fever. I thought of how I enjoyed teaching and how I loved to bring joy to people lives. I just had to figure out a lucrative career that would allow me to do that. One that I would be happy in. My professional woes switched and I began to think of my personal problems. How could I have allowed myself to become so vulnerable, so weak? I hurt Michael and I hurt myself. Where did my rules go, where did my stability go? I thought about how I threw everything away for Montel. How I had jeopardized everything. For what? Montel was still married and I was still alone. After hours of pondering away at my mistakes, I built up enough courage to call him. I left a message on his beeper in hopes that he would really hear me and understand where I was coming from.

"Montel, it's me. What happened tonight was a huge mistake. One that I will forever regret. Tonight I realized all the hurt and pain loving you has caused, and I just can't do it anymore. I can't see you anymore. As long as you are married, there is no chance of us. So please hear me when I say this, goodbye."

I hung up as I heard the beeping sound that let me know my message was sent. I hope he doesn't call or come by. I don't know if I can face him head on. What we did was wrong. He still had his wife, but I had no one. I knew I couldn't smooth things over with Michael, he probably held nothing but contempt for me. So I sat in my room with all the lights turned off. I thought about how much love I witnessed in one day. The love Raymond had for Tasha. The love between Lisa and Damon. I thought of Tanya and her husband, and then my mother and father. I ached for a relationship like that. Unconditional love. I thought I had that with Montel, but how could I? He was married and I was the other woman.

As much as it hurt me to think of myself like that, I did. I always thought of myself as the girlfriend, wifey material. I thought about Jennifer and her sweet and kindhearted face that made me hate myself even more. She seemed so nice, so loving. That image stayed in my head. I made it a point that every time I thought of Montel, I would think of Jennifer's face and that would make me stop. For that image had made me sick with guilt and I didn't think of myself so highly anymore. I thought of myself as nothing. That was a feeling I wasn't used to, and did not ever want to entertain.

CHAPTER TWENTY-ONE

Months went by. No calls from Montel. No calls from Michael. I hadn't seen either of them since the night little Raymond was born. Christmas rolled around and I heard nothing from them. New Year's Eve came around and still I had heard nothing. Valentine's day crept up on me, still neither one had called me. I spent my holidays with family. I helped Tasha out with the baby; she didn't know a thing about babies. Tasha started wedding plans for them of course. She was so excited.

I had made some New Years resolutions of course that I wanted to stick by. Start my own business, lose like ten pounds, and get over Montel. Not a day went by that I didn't think about him. Every lonely night I reminisced on what we had. I thought about how I hurt Michael and wished he were still around. Above all, Michael was my friend. We should have stayed that way. Nonetheless, I had not been serviced in three months. My well was running dry.

I spent all my time trying to figure out how to start my new business. I figured out that during those Lamaze classes, I really enjoyed the teaching and positive responses. My classes started to fill up and before I knew it, instead of two times a week, I was teaching classes four times a week. I got such positive responses from mothers who had given birth and referred me to friends and family.

One woman wrote me a thank you card: *"Sasha, I just want to say thank you so much. My labor was 23 hours and you would think my pain was unbearable. I did the relaxation techniques you taught us and it was like I was in a trance. My mind, body, and soul felt like they were one and the pain was shut out. I am not saying there wasn't any pain, but your relaxation methods got me through it. I hope I didn't write too much. Thank you again. Lena Richards. P.S. You should really think about broadening your classes, they would benefit so many women."*

With that note, the inspiration came. T helped me a lot since she was a successful businesswoman. She was so excited for me, and so proud too. I created my own web page and made some business cards. I got some good referrals from my former colleagues at Boston General. I was on a roll.

At first it started off slow, then after three months the volume picked up. My classes fit ten couples, $300 bucks a pop, two nights a week for four weeks of training. My business started booming. Once I put the thank you letters people sent me on the web and in the newspaper. I was on a roll. Every class was full. I was booked through June! If business continued this way, I'd need to lease out a building to teach the class in instead of using the YMCA, that a friend of a friend let me use.

Financially, things were looking up. It wasn't a physician's salary, but it was something to pay the bills and leave me plenty to spare. I cut down my living expenses. I sold my BMW, did a few yard sales, pawned some unnecessary jewelry and other things. I got used to this income cut real fast.

I was happy though, happier than I had ever been. I didn't have a man in my life though. I met a fella here and there but nothing that led to more than one phone call. I was becoming content with the fact that I might end up alone. I had to learn how to cope if I was going to make it. I got so tired of hearing family and even strangers say, “A pretty girl like you should have a man in her life. Where’s all the romance, Sasha? Where’s your man?” Damn it people, I didn’t have one! It wasn’t my fault that men were dick heads!

For instance, I met this fella named Sean. I went to the movies alone, something I never did. After the movies, I walked down Newbury Street to window shop. Sean was leaning on a 2002 Lexus GS400, silver with tinted windows. I walked by him as if I didn’t notice him at all. He stopped me and said, “Hey, how you doing?”

I said, “Fine.”

We proceeded to talk, and exchanged numbers. He got my cell phone number of course. He gave me his cell and his home number. He called the next day wanting to hook up, “the when you coming over routine.” First off, I couldn’t stand a man whose first words were “When you coming over?” To me, that meant “When you letting me hit that?” So from there, I knew what Sean was after. I contemplated it though, seeing how I hadn’t been serviced in a while. I left it up to chance.

Finally, after two weeks of conversation, I met him on Michelle’s street. I didn’t want him to know where I lived. He could be another psycho, like Jason. I parked my car, jumped in his, and we drove off. To my surprise we went to pick up his friend. I thought to myself, is this a date? His friend Earl jumped in the car. I was introduced, and that was that. Three stops later, Earl asked did I smoke weed? I said occasionally, and this could be one of those occasions. So we went to Malcolm X Park, smoked two blizzes, and talked for a while. I felt like I was hanging out with my girls. It was good because I didn't feel the pressures of dating. It was a cool atmosphere. It was also bad, because I was used to the royal treatment at my age, not this high school shit.

As I thought about it, high school times were so much simpler. The dude you wanted to talk to was a couple of classrooms over. Seeing him in the hall was like heaven. At lunchtime you would always put on a show, just in case he was watching. You would ride the train to the movies, play video games at his house. Smoke trees together, chill, and try to explore each other's body. Damn, I missed those days. Things were just too complicated now. There were too many choices, too many ifs, ands, and buts.

Anyways, I got hungry so I asked Sean could we go get something to eat. I asked Sean, not Earl. It was time for Earl to go home. We got in the car. Sean had the nerve to ask Earl what he was going to do.

Earl said, "I don't know, I am kind of hungry too."

I said, "Sean let's go get something to eat. Where you live Earl?"

If Sean didn't get that hint, I might just have to be blunt. Sean got the hint. Earl didn't. But best believe Sean dropped Earl off at his house and we went to Boston House of Pizza. While ordering, Sean's pager went off, he said he would be right back. The food was ready. It came up to $17.98. Sean was still on the phone, so I paid for the food. I sat down started to eat my food, still no Sean.

After about a good fifteen minutes Sean came back into the shop, and said, "Oh damn the food is ready, let's go."

I was eating, stuffing my face. I looked at him like he was crazy.

"How much did the food come up to?" he asked.

I told him. I also told him I wasn't finished eating and suggested we eat here. Sean was still persistent. He wanted to go.

I said, "Who were you talking to all that time while you're here with me?"

"Oh, it was my little sister's birthday."

Please, the smile that man had on his face when he came back from the phone was no smile from talking to a sibling. It was a smile that he was getting up with someone else tonight besides me. I brushed off his lie and proceeded to eat my food.

He said, "Well, I'll be in the car."

I was disgusted and lost my appetite, but still stayed in the pizza shop, just for spite. See this is why I don't even deal with dudes the same age as me. They are so immature. How rude was this dude to leave me alone twice, in the pizza shop after I paid for our food? This night was over. After spending like another fifteen minutes in the pizza shop, I went outside. I got in Sean's Lexus, and didn't say a word. He asked me if I wanted to go to his house.

I said, "Negative, and bring me to my car."

He was silent for a minute, and then said, "Why are you silent all of a sudden? I know you aren't sweating me over any punk eighteen dollars."

I felt like saying, nigga do you see these shoes I am wearing, Prada? Do you see the matching bag, one and half platinum diamond earrings and Movado watch with diamonds bezels on me? Do I look like I am worried about 18 punk dollars? I said nothing though. Silence kills them even worse. He didn't say anything, just kept sighing all the way to Michelle's house.

He pulled up and said, "Yo, if it's the money you're worried about, I got you."

I felt like saying, I haven't been worried about such a small debt since I used to spot one of my girls for a forty ounce of Old English and three bottles of Boones Farms. I said nothing though, just proceeded to get out of his car.

He stopped me and said, "Damn, is it like that? What you going to do tonight? You want to come to my house?"

He asked me again, I can't even fathom the idea of your cheap ass, no class, and low-life dick in me. I said nothing, got in my car, slammed the door, proceeded to start my engine and forget I even met this clown. As I was getting in, he had the nerve to say, "Thanks for dinner." If I had a bottle, I would have thrown it. I just counted my blessings that I didn't have to deal with this shit on a regular basis anymore. To me, it seemed like men just didn't know what I wanted. They didn't have the *je ne sais quoi*, quality I was looking for. Who was I kidding, none of them held a candle to Montel. He was my standard for all men. To date anything less was a crime.

It was Saturday. Two weeks from now Raymond and Tasha were getting married. I was happy for Raymond, and scared for him at the same time. I didn't trust Tasha ever since that night she was on the phone with some no-name person. I felt something was off about her. I kept that to myself though. I didn't want Raymond to think I was jealous or envious of his relationship. If Tasha was doing wrong, she would be found out, one way or another. More and more, to me it seemed like she was all about the money.

Raymond and I had fronted the bill for this wedding. Her father was supposed to chip in; we are still waiting for the check. I know one thing, if that check doesn't come, there will be no photographer or video man. It will just be me with my disposable camera and camcorder. It was a small wedding though, about a hundred guests. The cost was under $5,000, so it wasn't that bad.

Through these months, I learned how to budget. This indeed was going to be a budget, shot-gun wedding. Tasha asked me to pick up her dress because she was busy doing little last minute things. I faked like I liked her, waiting for her slip up, because liars always do. I should have felt bad about my feelings toward her, but I didn't. Maybe I was jealous and envious. Maybe if I was planning my own wedding, I wouldn't be so harsh.

Whatever. I was still being that fake bitch. I picked up Tasha's dress at David's Bridal in Dedham. It seemed like I hadn't been out there in a while. Montel and I used to go to the movies out there, shop, and then eat. As memories crept up on me, I wandered into the restaurant Montel used to take me to for brunch on Saturday afternoon. I sat down by myself and ordered. I missed him, but I would never tell him that.

After feeling empty, I left the restaurant. On my way to the car, I heard someone shouting my name. I knew the voice, however I didn't want to turn around.

Montel came up on me like a speeding car. "Sasha you didn't hear me calling you? Yeah, you did. What's up how have you been?"

"I am fine and yourself?"

"Doing good, real good, I miss you."

Oh here we go. I had to fight my emotions, try to stick by everything I had been saying. I couldn't though. I was dancing inside, so happy to see him, and I didn't want to let him go. "Who you out here with, your wife?"

"No." Montel shook his head when he said that. "I'm just chilling, enjoying this nice spring day. What about yourself?"

"I'm picking up Tasha's dress. Raymond and her are getting married."

"Oh really, they in love?"

"They appear to be."

Montel's face turned serious, "Well I hope so, because a marriage without love is doomed."

I felt he wanted me to go deeper into his comment, but I didn't. I wanted to know what he meant by that, but I left it alone.

"Well nice seeing you," I said as I proceeded to walk away.

He grabbed my arm and said, "Can I call you sometime?"

I wanted so bad to say sure, instead I said, "Call me for what? Our lives are in two different directions. The past is the past. Let's just leave it at that."

Montel let my arm go, just as he had let me go before. I left. I couldn't get out of there fast enough. I felt like crying but I didn't, I held back the tears.

I reached home and there was a series of messages on my answering machine. Mostly hang-ups. I tried to match the numbers on my caller ID, but they were all unavailable. Lisa left me a message to go see Michelle. She needed us. T left me a message saying it was important that I talk to her. A few sign-ups for my Lamaze class. Aunt Mimi, wanting to go over last minute details for the wedding. Finally, a message from Tasha asking if I could watch Little Raymond for her. She needed to go over a few things with her cousin for the wedding.

I called Raymond. He was upstairs with the baby and I told him I would baby-sit, so he could go to work and Tasha could do whatever. I was about to go upstairs when something dawned on me. I looked at my caller ID, Sean Moss. Sean's number was on my caller ID, 617-555-3876. I never gave that boy my number; he only had my cell phone number. Could he have been the one calling and hanging up? I sat and thought things out. The last number on my caller ID was his. The last message on my answering machine was from Tasha, same time. My imagination went wild. I decided to call Sean. The phone rang, a girl's voice picked up. It sounded like Tasha, but I wasn't sure. Couldn't make accusations if I wasn't sure. So I tried to disguise my voice and began, "Who is this? Where is Sean?"

The voice came through the phone, "No who the fuck is this calling my man?"

That was Tasha for sure, but I needed more info. I started to play along, "Where's Sean? This is Lisa."

"Lisa who?" Tasha replied.

"Lisa who wants to speak to Sean."

"Whatever, don't be calling here for my man, bitch!"

Tasha hung up. I called back, my number was blocked, Tasha yelled out some fuck you bitches and other curse words and kept hanging up. Finally after like five times calling back, Sean answered the phone. "Who is this?"

"What's up, Sean? This is Sasha."

"I thought you weren't going to call me anymore." I could hear Tasha yelling in the background.

"I changed my mind, but I guess I should have kept it simple because I see you are with the next chick."

Sean said coldly, "Well you were acting funky about your loot, so I left it at that."

"I see. Can you do me a favor, Sean?"

"What?"

"Put Tasha on the phone. Tell her it's Sasha Freeman, Raymond's sister. She'll know."

Sean shut up like he knew Raymond and the whole situation. Tasha jumped on the phone, still thinking I was Lisa, the other woman, trying to cuss me out.

I said, "Tasha, do you know who this is?"

Tasha said, "Yeah, the bitch that keeps calling my man."

"No honey, this is your soon-to-be sister-in-law, Sasha. I just have one question for you, are you coming to get your things or should Raymond throw them out?"

Tasha hung up.

I called Raymond before she could and told him to come down here immediately. He came with the baby. I told him what happened. Of course, he didn't believe me, so I had him call the number. No answer, I figured as much. I said call Tasha's cousin to see if she was there. No answer there either. I tried to convince Raymond, but he wouldn't hear it. He kept asking me if I was sure it was her, was I positive. I gave him the facts, but still he was in denial. If only I knew where Sean lived, we could go over there. I recalled he said something about Maywood Street in one of our conversations. I didn't know the house, but I knew where the street was. If Tasha's car was parked out front, then Raymond would know.

We dropped off the baby over to Aunt Mimi's house. She wanted to know what was going on, I told her I'd tell her later. We reached the street. Tasha's car wasn't parked on the street, but her cousin's car was.

Raymond began to convince himself, "See her cousin is probably over there, and they were just fooling with you. You know how you girls do."

I shook my head. "I know what I'm talking about."

Raymond was ready to go. I wasn't. We argued for ten minutes. Then, just as we were about to pull off, Tasha came out, got into her cousin's car, and drove off. Raymond looked clueless.

"Do you want to go inside?" I asked.

"Hell yeah!" He replied.

We rang Sean's bell. He answered with no surprise. He said in a smirk kind of way, "Your girl just left."

Raymond's fist began to ball.

I asked, "Are you seeing Tasha, Sean?"

"Yeah, I been seeing her for a minute. Yo money, if you ask me, she is just a trick- ass bitch. No one to fight over."

Raymond's face was on fire, ready to crush Sean into little pieces. I pulled his elbow and persuaded him to let it go.

Sean said, "Hey, Sasha, call me sometime."

I turned and said, "I don't think so."

Raymond was silent on the way home. I felt for him. When you find out the one you love isn't, your whole world is crushed. It was worst for Raymond because this was his first love and they had a son together. He tricked around with so many women that it was ironic his love would trick on him.

I said, "Raymond, I know how you feel. Trust me, I been there. It takes time, just don't do anything crazy."

Raymond let out a huff. "Crazy? You haven't seen crazy. Pass me your phone, Sasha."

Raymond called Aunt Mimi, told her to watch the baby, would explain later. She agreed. I called the locksmith to change some locks. Once we got home, Tasha still wasn't there. I guessed she would try to wait it out. I helped Raymond pack up her things. The locksmith changed the locks. The phone rang. Raymond answered. It was Tasha. He was calm at first, then all of a sudden he whaled on her. I could hear her cursing through the phone. I guess she realized he didn't believe her, so she started yelling? Raymond told her not to come by here, the locks were changed, lil Raymond was at his aunt's house, and her stuff was about to be dropped off. Tasha didn't sound like she was going for that. Raymond hung up on her. He looked more upset than he did on the phone, like she said something to break him.

"Raymond, what's wrong?" I asked.

"You know what the chick had the nerve to say to me? She said Little Raymond isn't mine. What kind of shit is that? You get caught up, and then try to throw more salt to the wound. She is sick. Fuck her, that baby is my son."

I tried to reason with him, and the possibilities, but he wouldn't listen. I tried to convince him to let me drop off her stuff, but he wanted to go. I asked him to promise me that he wouldn't do anything stupid. He promised, but I was still worried.

After Raymond left, I called the only person who could help me, Michael. It had been months since we had spoken, months since that night. I thought time would heal some of that, I hoped so. I didn't get him. I got his answering machine. "Michael, this is Sasha. I know we haven't spoken since, well, you know. I'm not calling for me, though, I'm calling for Raymond. He just found out some disturbing things about Tasha and he's dropping her stuff off at her cousin's house. He wouldn't let me go with him, so I was wondering if, oh never mind, I can't keep running to you with my problems. Sorry, forget it. Just erase this message." I hung up. Something came over me when I was leaving that message. I felt vulnerable, exposed. I didn't like it.

Hours went by, no word from Raymond. The phone rang; I hoped it was Raymond with good news. It wasn't. It was Montel with old news. I asked why he was calling. He said I knew.

"Don't play games, Montel, what do you want? I thought we settled this."

"You told me not to call you unless I wasn't married. So I'm calling you."

A long pause took over.

"Montel what are you saying?"

"I'm out, I am done. Jennifer and I are divorced. I tried to make it work, but it just isn't. I needed a friend to talk to, aren't we still friends?"

I paused, scared of my next response. "Yeah, we're still friends."

I bounced back on my sofa, like weights had been lifted off my feet. Montel asked about Raymond and Tasha. I went into detail, as if Montel and I had never stopped talking. As we made small talk, I hoped that this time would be different, that we could be together finally. All my doubts stayed present, as well as my fears. I knew though, if I never got the chance to see what we were really made of, how would I know if he really was or wasn't the one? I kept on talking and kept on hoping.

CHAPTER TWENTY-TWO

Once again, Montel and I were back on. The first week, dinner and a movie. The second week, dinner and a movie at my place. The third week, Montel was back in my bed. We spent all possible time together; we were doing our love thing. He helped me out with some business ideas. I encouraged him to stay in his son's life. On nights that he would stay at my place, he would get up early in the morning to take his son to daycare. I never once complained about that. I never discouraged him from seeing his son. If anything, I encouraged him to do right by his son. Since he was still a baby, it was easier and he didn't have to explain now. I looked forward to meeting his son one day, whenever Montel was ready. I planned to be in Montel's life forever, so that meant loving his son as much as I could. I didn't have a problem with that at all.

Sometimes, I thought about Jennifer and what she was going through. It dawned on me that she slept with him when she knew he was with me. I didn't have much sympathy for her after I thought about that. She didn't seem like that type of woman though. The sneaky kind of woman who will get what she wants when she wants, no matter who gets hurt. That kind of woman didn't fit the person I met in Jennifer. Nonetheless, I didn't let her marital woes stop me from being happy. I was on cloud ninety-nine. Montel and I were in love, and loving every moment of it.

At the end of July, I would have one week for a break between Lamaze classes, so Montel and I planned a trip together. Hawaii was our destination. He planned the trip, every last detail.

He showed me the brochure. I was impressed. Things were going good in my life, too good. I held on to whatever happiness I had, because who knew when this would stop and when or if, happiness like this would ever return to my door. I tried not to be snowed under Montel's spell, but it was so easy. Loving him was too easy.

My phone rang. I answered, another hang up. This was like the fifth hang up during the week. I got hang ups like this for a month now. I thought it was Tasha or Sean, since he had my number now. But when I thought about it, these hang ups started before that shit went down with Tasha. If this continued, I would have to change my number. Speaking of Tasha, Raymond still wouldn't agree to a blood test. As far as he was concerned Little Raymond was his son. I tried to talk some sense in him, but he wouldn't listen. Tasha was going to take him to the cleaners on child support. Raymond worked two jobs, under the court's eyes, lived rent free, and had trouble with the law. The court would gladly grant Tasha full custody and give her half of Raymond's paycheck. I tried explaining that to Raymond, but he said he was going to do right by his son, even if that meant dealing with Tasha. So, Tasha's money- hungry ass put in a request to garnish Raymond's wages for a child he's not sure is even his. I wanted to ring Tasha's neck. I would have if Raymond did not personally ask me to stay out of it. He was his own man and would take care of his affairs. I don't know what has gotten into him. When I see him, we are going to have to go over this one more time, because he can't be serious about this shit. No way. No how. My phone rang again. It was Michelle. "Girl where have you been? I have been leaving message after message for weeks."

"Michelle, I have tried to reach you too, but you're never home. No one comes by to see me, what's up?"

"I need you to come by my house, we need to talk pronto."

"All right, I just have to make a few calls. I'll w be over in a minute."

I made it to Michelle's house in like half an hour. She was sitting on her porch drinking a cup of lemonade. I hugged her and said, "What up girlfriend, long time don't see."

"Yeah, you've been missing in action for a while now."

"I haven't been avoiding anyone. I just was keeping to myself, that's all."

"Who are you kidding, Sasha? I know what's going on"

I thought *damn it! I was going to get around to telling you guys about Montel, I just didn't know how.* I began to start my story, when Michelle interrupted me.

"You feel left out, because you are the only one without a man?"

She caught me off guard with that one.

"We're still your girls, Sasha. Just because we have men, doesn't mean we can't spend time with you and kick it like we used to."

I thought *you are so way off base. Little do you know my love life is better than it could ever be.* I wanted to tell Michelle that. I wanted to tell her the truth. I just nodded my head and went along with whatever she thought was the reason I hadn't been around much. The real reason was, between Raymond's drama, my new business, and Montel, I just didn't have the time to shoot the breeze.

"I called you over here for two reasons. One was to tell you that I miss you and I'm sure Lisa and T do too. The other reason was, I need your cousin Tanya's number, so she can hook me up with a good lawyer."

I looked baffled, "Lawyer?"

"Oh, so you don't know? Jamal and I are getting a divorce."

I paused. I was shocked and gleeful at the same time. I questioned, "A divorce, what happened?"

Michelle shook her head, and said, "What didn't happen?"

She laughed a bit, but it wasn't a cheerful laugh. It was a sad one. She began to tell me her story. I listened with open ears.

"After all this time I've been with Jamal, all the drama he has brought my way, I never thought he would bring it to our home. I never thought he would bring it to my children. Jamal doesn't respect himself; therefore, he can't possibly respect anyone else. I went away three weekends ago. My mother took me to a weekend spa. Jamal agreed to watch the children. I really didn't want him to. I called you but you weren't around, so I gave in. Jamal was actually excited about me going away. My mother and I went to the spa and had a lovely time. I was so relaxed in one day that I decided to go home. I still was uneasy about leaving the kids alone with Jamal. When I got home, Jamal acted very surprised and very uneasy to see me. He was sitting at the table drinking a beer. He started asking me stupid questions like, what does it smell like in here or if I can go to the store and get him some more beers? I agreed. One, because I felt so good from the spa, and two, I was happy he didn't burn down the house while I was gone. So Jamal tried to rush me out the door before I even put my jacket on. I stopped him and told him that I wanted to check on the kids first. He tried to steer me away from their room. I got anxious because he didn't want me to see the kids. I yanked his arm off me, and went to their rooms. They were peacefully asleep. I looked at him like what is your problem? So after I checked on the kids, I got ready to go to the store. I was on my way out the door when I heard a noise coming from the kid's room. I figured one of them must have awakened, so I went to check. Jamal was on my trail. I got in their room and they were still asleep. As I left the kids room, I noticed a shadow on the wall. The shadow did not belong to me, Jamal, or the kids. I turned and there was a half-naked woman in my children's closet. I snatched her up out of the closet. No explanation was needed. She was there in my house fucking my husband, with my kids in the next room. I don't know what Jamal told her and I didn't care. I threw her out with just her panties and bra on. Jamal looked bewildered like he didn't know what to say. I paused for a minute, and then began to kick his ass. I threw him out too. The next day, I threw all his shit in the trash. I cleaned house."

I looked at Michelle, so full of life; once again so full of joy. Once again, she had done the unthinkable. She cleared the snow from her head and began to see clearly.

"Did you know the girl?"

"No, probably some random affair. She looked young though, about nineteen. She had these innocent eyes. Her eyes reminded me of mine when I first met Jamal. Excited, naive, and happy. Now look at my eyes. Tired, weary and sad. I can only blame myself for letting Jamal get the best of my years, but I will not be taken anymore. I have a higher purpose now, and Jamal and I don't have any purpose at all. It took me a long time to realize that I can do bad all by myself. I may end up alone without a man in my life, but when I think about it, I have been doing that for the past ten years. I envy you, Sasha."

"Why?" I asked her. "I don't have a man either."

"True, but you do fine without them, and you know that. You left Montel alone, which had to be hard. You chose you over him. That's why I envy you."

I felt like a fake. I didn't want to spoil all of Michelle's empowerment, so I pretended and went along with whatever she was saying. After our conversation, I was about to leave when Michelle stopped me and told me the second thing she had to talk to me was about T.

"I thought you already told me what you had to say?"

"Oh yeah, I must have snuck something extra in. Nonetheless, have you spoken with T?"

I shook my head. "She left me a message, but every time I call her she's never there."

"You have to find her. I think she's in trouble."

"Why do you say that?"

"Well a couple of weeks ago Ricky got divorced from his wife."

"Isn't that a good thing?" I asked.

"Yeah, it would have been good, if Ricky was doing it for T, but he was doing it for himself."

I was confused.

"Look, Sasha, you need to find T and talk some sense into her before she does something crazy."

From Michelle's voice I figured that whatever she knew about Ricky and T wasn't good and I had to catch up with T as soon as possible.

As I was leaving, Michelle also said, "Oh yeah, I saw Montel the other day."

I turned around and tried to show no interest, "Oh yeah where?"

"He was at the supermarket with his wife."

I started to correct Michelle and tell her that they weren't married anymore, but I would have to explain how I knew. Since I wasn't in the mood for confession, I brushed it off and went on my mission to find T.

After eight phone messages and some information from T's parents, I found her. She was on Martha's Vineyard, at one of her hotels. Why hadn't she called any of us? What was going on? I caught the next ferry to the Vineyard to find out what was going on with T. I got to the hotel, asked for Tameika Williams. The staff looked at me like I was crazy.

"Look, I know she's here, just tell me where she is please."

The staff still looked at me like I was speaking French.

"Should I do a room-to-room search for Ms. Williams or what?"

"She doesn't wish to be disturbed," this feminine fellow said to me.

I said, "Oh well, she's going to be disturbed and you are too, if I don't get some satisfaction in this place!"

He-she rolled his eyes and pointed to the door as if I was going to leave. I stood my ground.

He-she said, "Look, let's not have to call security, girlfriend, just leave quietly and I will forget this."

"I dare you to call security, because I am not leaving until I talk to Tameika."

He-she rolled his eyes and sucked his teeth and proceeded to call security. The other desk clerk stopped him and motioned for me to follow her.

She whispered, "You are Sasha, right? T's friend? Just go outside around the back and I'll let you into her room, I'm worried about her and glad to see you here."

With that last comment, I was worried too. I did what the petite young lady said and she let me into T's room.

The room was dark, curtains closed, and messy with empty pizza boxes covering the glass coffee table. I still didn't see T. The bathroom door was closed. The room was so quiet, so still. I opened the bathroom door. A trail of clothes, empty champagne bottles, and a blunt burning a hole in the bathroom rug led to T's body in a tub full of water. I was frantic. I ran up to her. Her entire head was submerged. I quickly lifted her head from under the cold water. She was heavy, dead weight. I struggled to get her to the floor. I yelled her name, screaming for her to wake up and say she was all right.

I yelled, "Somebody help me!"

I checked her pulse. Weak. She wasn't breathing. I began mouth-to-mouth resuscitation. Tears rolled down my face as I tried to revive her and yell for help, at the same time. A million thoughts raced through my head. How? Why? What did she do to herself? By now, no one had heard my cry and I felt like I had exhaled a hundred breaths into T's breathless body. It felt hopeless. I smacked her face and yelled. "Wake up, wake up, you better wake up or I will kill you!"

I gave her two more breaths, crying the whole time. Just when all was silent and all was still, I heard choking. T threw up in my face. She was awake, she was breathing. I lost a liter of tears as I hugged her. T was in a daze.

After I got T something to wear, some food, and something to drink, we didn't talk for hours. We sat in the hotel room not saying a word. She turned on the TV and started flipping channels. By now I was getting annoyed and had a list of questions for her, but I didn't know where to start. I know one thing, I wasn't leaving her alone, and I wasn't leaving without her. T continued to flip through the channels.

I sipped my tea and said, "So you want to talk about it or what? I am not leaving here until we do, so you might as well start explaining yourself."

With an attitude T said, "Talk about what?"

I looked at her like she had lost it. "I don't know. We can talk about why you are here, and why I found you in your bathroom half dead."

T smirked, "I wasn't half nothing. I don't know what you're talking about. I don't even know why you're here, personally."

"Whatever, T you can zigzag around the issue all you want, but I need to know what's going on. Where's Ricky?"

T laughed. "Don't know, don't care."

"Well obviously something is wrong or you wouldn't be trying to kill yourself."

"What!" T yelled. "I don't know what you are talking about."

"So, are you trying to tell me that I just didn't find you in a tub full of water, unconscious?"

"I must of fell asleep in the tub."

"Yeah right. You were highly drunk, highly high, and out of control. You tried to hurt yourself didn't you?"

T was silent.

"Should I call Ricky and find out from him what the deal is?"

T let out another laugh. "If you can find him."

"What's that supposed to mean? Did you do something to Ricky?"

"Oh, now you're worried about Ricky?"

"I'm worried about you, now what happened?"

T let out a long huff. "It's over. We are over."

I paused. "You tried to kill yourself over some nigga?"

T was silent. She began to roll a blunt.

"Don't you think you have had enough for one day?" I scolded her.

"I've had enough for a lifetime."

"T, what's up?"

T sparked the blunt and began to tell her melancholy story. With one exhale of smoke she began. "Ricky got divorced. I thought, after the divorce, I was going to be with him forever. He put up the front like it was going to be that way. Well, two weeks ago the divorce was finalized. I was jumping up and down. He was calm and silent. He asked me if I could give him some space, you know, to work out what he was feeling emotionally. I gave him hell, but eventually I saw his point and caved in. A week went by, I didn't hear from him. Just when I was about to lose it, he called me at midnight for a booty call. After the deed was said and done, his pager went off. He checked his message and came back to bed. I asked him who would be paging him so late? He brushed it off and told me it was his wife. So the next morning he got up real early and told me he had a meeting or something and would call me later. By now I'm feeling real insecure, real insignificant in his life. I started tripping, talking to myself, and trying to make sense of his recent attitude change toward me. I picked up the phone to call you and get my head straight. I looked on the phone's display screen and noticed that Ricky left his pager's code on the display box. Now I had his code. I fought trying to check his messages, but I couldn't. I started dialing, something I wished I hadn't done."

T ticked off on her fingers. "First saved message: *Ricky baby where are you? I miss you. Call me when you get home, Joselyn.* The next saved message: *Ricky, you know you wrong. Call me when you get in. I have to talk to you about something, Angel.* The next saved message: *Boo, for real, I don't like the way things are going with us. You haven't called me since your divorce and I'm trying to see you. I thought it was going to be me and you. Call Daria when you get a chance.* There were like ten saved messages, all from ten different women. Ricky was playing his wife and me the whole time. I thought I knew what he needed. I thought I knew him. All the plans we made, all the promises. Promises he didn't have to make. I let Linc go, I let my life go, all for him. I just knew it was going to be him and me. One girl left some message late last night, the message he said his wife left. LIAR! I was dating a gigolo. I couldn't think. I lost it. I changed the code to his beeper so he couldn't retrieve any more messages. I paged him to my house several times, but e didn't return one page. The least thing he could do was face me. After not hearing from him, I started tripping. I drank and I drank. I smoked and I smoked. Nothing helped, nothing kept me unfeeling. I tried to call you guys, but I couldn't. I couldn't face the embarrassment, the 'I told you so'. I came out here last week to think and try to sort things out. I don't know what happened to me. I don't know where I went wrong."

T was silent, apparently trying to make sense of her actions and not succeeding. I thought she didn't know what feelings did her in. She was strong, but not strong enough to face defeat. Not strong enough to realize she was ten times as important than Ricky. She apologized for herself. I didn't know what to say. I asked, "So where is Ricky now?"

"I don't know."

"Well, he isn't going to get away with this shit, no way, no how. Call him now to my phone."

"Why?"

"Just call him and tell him you have a surprise waiting for him out here. Tell him you've been busy. Don't even act like you're mad."

T paged him. Surprised, he called back hesitantly, and agreed to meet T there. T sounded so sweet, so loving over the phone that any man couldn't resist. Two hours later, the desk called and said he was here. After cleaning up the room, I got something sexy for T to wear, popped open some champagne, threw rose petals on the bed, and prepared a bubble bath. Then, I hid in the closet with a tape recorder.

Ricky entered. T worked her magic. She got him undressed and in the tub. She then tied him to each knob in the tub. Ricky looked so erotic, so vulnerable and pleased with T's performance. Just when he thought all was good, T slapped him, illed on him, and told him what she knew. He tried to deny it. T turned on the hair dryer and threatened to throw it in the tub if he didn't tell her the truth. He confessed about all his women, his ex-wife, and his new fiancé, Nyesha. I thought that last confession would send that hair dryer straight in the tub and shock his butt.

T held on strong, and said with a long breath, "Did you get all that Sasha?" Ricky looked confused.

I came out of hiding and said, "Yup."

T dared to throw the dryer in the tub as Ricky begged for forgiveness. The man was crying. T let out a vengeful laugh. I let out a couple of giggles too. I was uneasy because I didn't know if T was going to electrocute him or what. T looked at me, looked at herself in the mirror, then looked at Ricky.

"This is what you have made me do. Know that you brought this on yourself. Look at what you have done to me, reduced me to a murderer."

Ricky begged for his life. He cried. He pleaded. He was so sorry.

T leaned over about to drop the dryer in the tub. She said in a soft whisper, "But you know what, Ricky? You aren't even worth murdering. Ending your life like this would be too easy for you. You would never know your wrongs, and you would never suffer like you should."

T turned off the hair dryer as Ricky began his many thank yous. T left him in the bathroom. She hugged me and thanked me for being here.

I asked, "What do you want to do with the tape?"

"Lets make copies and send them to all the women Ricky knows."

On that note, we searched his pockets and found his little address book. Mostly all of the women's telephone numbers and addresses were in there. His precious Nyesha's was the first address we searched for. We cleaned up the room, took Ricky's clothes, and threw them out. Then we left. We left Ricky there with no clothes, no money, and no way to get back to Boston. T put a 'do not disturb' sign on the door and that was that. That would be the last time T heard or saw Ricky.

Weeks went by. I spent most of my time with friends. I made sure T and Michelle had the support they needed to move past their love hardships. I was happy with Montel. We had planned a trip to Hawaii next Saturday. This was going to be seven days of paradise. Just Montel, the islands, and me, that was all I wanted. I felt kind of guilty though, seeing how mostly everyone around me was so sad. I could only share my joy with Lisa. I told her about Montel. No one else knew. She gave me her reservations about him, but still tried to support my decision to continue to see him. People can change and this trip to Hawaii proved that.

After packing my clothes, I checked on everyone before I left. Raymond had the weekend off. He was going to spend time with his son. I stopped trying to win that battle with Raymond. He believed that was his son, and that was the end of it. Tasha, of course, was content, as long as the checks kept coming. I was disgusted by the whole situation, but I was a firm believer that those who do wrong, get done wrong eventually. So, Tasha will get hers, just like Ricky got his, and Jamal got his. I wasn't worried. I was too happy to be worried about anything. Montel had agreed to meet me at the airport. I showed my ID to the clerk and she looked me up, and proceeded to give me my ticket. She smiled at me, and I smiled back at her. I was feeling so good that day, feeling on top of the world. I waited for Montel at the gate. Our flight left at 10 a.m., it was 9:15 a.m. No sign of Montel. He was just running a little late, I thought. I began to read my Vibe magazine as I waited for Montel. Fifteen minutes went by. Passengers began to board the plan, still no sign of Montel. I began to get worried. What if something happened to him, I thought. 10 a.m., the plan left, Montel was still not there, and I was left there, still wondering what was going on. I walked out of that airport, without the smile I came in with. I didn't even have enough energy to tell the clerk my luggage was on board. I pulled out my cell phone, and paged Montel. I didn't hear from him, no call back, and no message. I wanted to cry sitting on that curb as I waited for my call back. Instead, I flagged a cab, as I held my cell phone in my hand, still waiting for my call back.

CHAPTER TWENTY-THREE

The mall was packed. I needed a new dress, a new pair of shoes, a bag, and a makeover from Mac's counter at Macy's. Yes, it was a good day. I was so surprised when the show called me. I think highly of myself, but still I feel like a regular Joe, not a celebrity. Wow, someone actually wanted to meet me, and give me a surprise on the Vicki Rake show. I normally don't watch talk shows, but ever since the show called me, I been watching it everyday, trying to get a feel for the audience and the topics. Yesterday, the show was about deadbeat dads, and the day before that it was about meeting a long-lost relative. The topics were not too scandalous, so it seemed like a respectable show. I was just hyped up about being on TV. I never have been on TV, except in middle school when the news decided to do a story about inner city youth performing Shakespeare. That was only for a second though, no close-ups or nothing. Anyway, I had to be dressed to the nines for my debut. Who knows how many phone numbers I would get after this show.

My personal life had been on shaky ground since Hawaii. It had been three months and I hadn't heard a word from Montel. I checked the newspapers everyday to make sure nothing happened to him. I paged him several times, no returns. His cell phone was off and his home number was disconnected. I started to write him a letter but didn't know where to send it. After a while I finally realized that I had been stood up, but had no idea why. Things were good between us. He had gotten a divorce, and we were making progress. I accepted his son, wanted to even meet him one day. Montel didn't like that idea, but I knew it would grow on him. I just didn't understand. What the fuck happened to us? I blamed myself for days that turned into weeks. The truth of the matter was that Montel stood me up. He made plans and cancelled without notice. I just hoped that he was all right wherever he was, so I could get the chance to kill him when I saw him.

Anyway, the show's taping was in two days. I invited Lisa, Michelle, and T to come along with me. The show was flying me in free, so I flew the ladies in with me. I had a hookup on airline tickets via a new friend.

As I was at the airport waiting for Montel's sorry ass, I guess one of the attendants took pity on me and tried to talk to me. He wrote down his number, I called after a week. His name was Paul. He was cool, but so not my type. After weeks and weeks of phone conversations and lunches, we decided to just be friends. He was pretty cool about it. That was the first male friend I made since Michael. Michael, I really messed things up with him. I didn't even try to redeem myself. I didn't call, I didn't write, I was wrong. But hey, I was in love with Montel, Michael knew that. He should have just kept it simple, instead of complicating things. I should have just held off and stayed his friend, not getting into a new relationship, when I was no way finished with the old one. Oh well, life lessons. I still wished Michael would call me, though.

Lisa was afraid to fly. She grabbed my arm every time the plane hit a little turbulence. I needed cocoa butter to smooth away the bruises on my arm. We were sitting in first-class seats, sipping on champagne at 10 in the morning, like true queens. We had not hung out like this in a while. Michelle was busy trying to pick her life back up after the divorce. T was trying to recover from her addiction to love. I was trying to convince myself that Montel was always wrong for me.

Lisa was sitting pretty in her relationship with Damon. To my surprise things were going so well between them. It has been like a year almost by my calculations. That was the longest Lisa had been in a relationship since Jake. They were so in love it was disgusting. He drove us to the airport, helped Lisa with the bags, walked with us to the check-in booth and even waited with us at the gate. Damn, could the brother give her some room? They hugged and kissed as we were leaving. I can't lie, I was jealous as hell. Through all this bullshit, Lisa found some love, with Damon, the "female entertainer". I was happy for her though, she deserved it. The rest of us were singing sad love songs. Lisa was singing happy ones. Maybe it was time for her to get a break, though. After dealing with Jake, she deserved something good in her life. She learned to let dogs lie where they may, a lesson the rest of us have learned slowly but surely. Whatever, I just felt lonely sometimes. But when I did I thought of what I did have, rather than what I didn't, and everything else seem to fall in place. I held on to the thought that, after all this heartache, my good times would come. They just had to, I thought.

After three glasses of wine, I started to settle in and start talking. The ladies also began to partake in the abyss of intoxication and start running their mouths about whatever came to mind.

T lifted up Lisa's arm while saying with a smirk, "Hey Lisa, where is Damon?"

Lisa grabbed her arm from T, as we all started laughing.

"Don't hate bitch,." Lisa said to T.

"Its cool, Lisa, you and Damon are doing y'all's love thing, that is peace, that's what's up," T replied.

"Yeah girl, hang on to him," Michelle added.

"Lisa, you do deserve some happiness, so take it while it is here, I added.

"I'll drink to that," Lisa agreed, while she held up her glass of wine and motioned for us to toast with her.

"So Sasha, who do you think wants to meet you?" Lisa asked.

"Well I think it's probably someone who has visited my website and is very impressed with my business. Or maybe it's an ex-flame who really would love to get back with me."

"Oh, someone like Michael?" Michelle added.

I almost choked on my wine. Michael, a name only I mentioned in silence. "Michael is so through with me, it isn't even funny. I screwed things up with him, I snowed him, and then did him wrong, like Montel did me."

"Please. Michael knew what he was working with, he should have seen that one coming," T said.

"True, but still, I could have prevented it from happening by just being honest with myself and with him."

"Whatever, no use crying over spilled milk, Sash, what's done is done. If it's meant to be, it will. I am so happy you gave up on Montel, he was such a loser," Lisa added.

Uh oh, a thought just crept up on me, no one knew about Montel and Hawaii, except Lisa. As far as they knew, I was done with him the night little Raymond was born. I wanted to come clean, but I thought, *what for?* I would just tell the same old story and hear the same old thing. It just didn't matter any more; some things were better left unsaid.

We arrived at the studio. Security escorted my girls to the audience. The producer came over to meet me and went over how things were going to go on the show. Next the director came in to discuss other things with me, such as rules and regulations. I had to sign some release form that I agreed to the taping. The makeup artist came in next. I explained to her that I didn't want a lot of makeup because I was already done up. Wardrobe came in; I was not interested in their outfits either. After all the preparations and such, I was lead to the room with some other guests who were going to be on the show as well. Finally, Vicki came in to meet the guests and gave her gratitude for us agreeing to be on the show. Vicki was much smaller in person; she seemed like a happy-go-lucky person. She made us feel relaxed, not pressured, and tried to coach us on how to behave on the show. She explained that the person, who wanted to meet us, would go out first, and then we would be signaled to come out and meet the person. We would be blind folded until we sat down next to the person. I was feeling kind of nervous at first, but I took another sip of wine that was in the show's waiting room, and I started feeling relaxed again. Vicki left us with that information then thanked us again for being on her show. She was really nice and down to earth. She didn't seem like the queen of scum that newspapers and critics mad her out to be. There were three other people waiting with me. I was the first one up. *Good*, I thought, *I can get this over with and go home.*

I tried to make small talk with the two young ladies who were waiting with me. The other fella seemed kind of distant and slow. I said, "Where are you girls from?"

The chubby black female, with a gold tooth, said, "I from Miami, what about you?"

"I'm from Boston."

"Boston?" she said with a surprised look. "There are black folks in Boston?"

I thought, *here we go again*. I got so tired of explaining to folks from the south that Boston is full of African Americans, more than they knew. I kept my composure though. "Yeah, there are plenty of African Americans in Boston. As a matter of fact, I brought my girls with me, and they're all black," I said to the gold-toothed Diva.

After that, I tried not to converse; she seemed kind of slow, too. I could hear the audience clapping as well as their "Oohs" and "Ahs", as whoever wanted to meet me was out on stage. I was so excited, I couldn't think who it could be. I just hoped it was some tall handsome brother who saw me somewhere but didn't have the courage to say anything to me. That would be so romantic. To bring me all the way out here in New York to meet me would be so sweet. I smiled at the thought.

The producer came into the room and signaled me to follow her. She blind folded me and led me onto the stage. My heart was racing, I was so nervous. I could feel the energy in the crowd, as if this was the moment of truth. I heard voices shouting, but they were muffled. I couldn't make out what they were saying. Something like, "Watch out girl!" I sat down and waited for my cue to take off my blindfold.

Vicki said "Hello, Sasha, you know that you are being brought to the show because someone wants to meet you."

I said, "Yes Vicki, I'm very anxious to see who wants to meet me."

Vicki said, "Okay, I'll let our guest begin. Go ahead, say hello."

"Hello, Sasha."

The voice sounded familiar, it was a female voice, no male, no cutie, I thought.

"Do you recognize the voice?" Vicki asked me.

"Kind of, I don't know who it is though."

The female guest said, "You know me, Sasha, just as I know you."

The squeaky voice, sent chills to my spine, I knew her. I swallowed as I began to undue my blindfold and face the music. I took my blindfold off, and to my terror, it was Jennifer, Montel's ex-wife.

The audience began to roar. A million thoughts went through my head. Why did she want to meet me, did she know about Montel and me? This outcome could not be good. Maybe she just wanted to thank me publicly for all I did for her. That last thought was stupid. The look on Jennifer's face meant war. I hope

Vicki hired extra security, because Jennifer looked like she was after my blood, and wouldn't be satisfied until I wasn't breathing.

Vicki said, trying to control the conversation. "Do you know each other, Sasha?"

"Yes, I know Jennifer."

"How do you know her Sasha?"

"She attended one of my Lamaze classes."

"Is that all?"

"Yes!" I said with conviction.

"Liar!" Someone yelled from the audience.

That was my cue, the shit had hit the fan, Jennifer knew. I started scanning the crowd looking for three familiar faces. Just then, I saw Lisa fanning her hand. I exhaled. If I was going down, at least I had my girls to back me up.

Vicki calmed the crowd down and began again. "Sasha, Jennifer tells us you know her husband."

I corrected Vicki. "I know Jennifer's ex-husband, Montel."

The audience roared.

"Wait." I said while putting my hands up trying to explain. "Montel and I go way back. Yes, I know Jennifer because she and Montel came to my Lamaaz class, but we used to date before that."

Jennifer barked, "Ex-husband, what do you mean ex? He still is my husband!"

I was dumb founded. I thought, *this girl is delusional.* The audience was taking over the sound; no one could hear my side of the story. I began to get aggravated.

Jennifer kept going on. "You are nothing but a two-dollar tramp! You had an affair with my husband; so don't try to deny it. You were sleeping with my man since we had our son."

The audience roared some more for Jennifer's side. I started to feel backed in a corner. Jennifer had the facts misconstrued, and she didn't know what was really going on. I tried to explain, but the audience drowned me out.

Vicki tried to take control back. "Sasha what do you have to say about this?"

I was pissed. "Vicki, first off I want to say, that I do not appreciate being dragged all the way to New York for this bullshit. This could have been handled just between you and me, Jennifer, over lunch."

The crowd snickered.

"Second of all, Jennifer, Montel was with me before you. You got pregnant while we were dating. He didn't even tell me he was getting married. I found out after the fact. As far as an affair going on between us, we were together one time during your marriage. We hooked up after your divorce." I crossed my arms as if I was through with this conversation.

Jennifer snapped back at me, "But we are still married so what the fuck are you talking about?"

The crowd roared to Jennifer's defense as if she broke me into little pieces. I was getting very annoyed with this whole situation.

"Well you know what, Ms. Jennifer, Montel assured me that you and him were finished, done, finis! I told him I was not seeing him while he was married, if he lied to me, then he lied to you too!" I rolled my eyes with that last comment.

Jennifer rolled her eyes at me. "Was this before or after you dropped your panties?"

The audience roared again.

I stood up. Jennifer was about to catch the serious smack down! No one was going to embarrass me on TV. "Look Bitch, you have the audacity to come up on this stage trying to look like Ms. Innocent. The truth of the matter is, you slept with my man on a one-night stand, got yourself pregnant, then trapped him into marriage. Now you want to come on TV to cry about being done wrong when you did yourself wrong. You are the slut, you are the sidekick, who threw your panties at my man when we were on the outs."

"What are talking about?" Jennifer looked confused.

"Montel and I were together at the beginning of last year until the spring. We got into an argument, I didn't hear from him in a week. In that week, you found your way into his bed, got yourself pregnant and forced him to marry you. He didn't want to marry you; he just wanted to do what was right. Montel loved me, but was torn between right and wrong, so there!"

"That is bullshit!" Jennifer snapped. "Montel and I have been together for the past five years."

I was caught off guard with that one. "Excuse me?"

"I've known Montel since we were teenagers. We hooked up when I was seventeen, broke up when he went to college, got back together when he moved to New York, and have been together ever since. So what are you talking about?" She responded.

This new information, I couldn't take standing up, I had to sit down. Her last words threw me for a loop. The only thing I could do was defend myself. "You are lying. I've known Montel since I was fifteen. We were together when he went to college. We broke up after I found him with some chick when I went to visit him in North Carolina. We got back together last year."

"You must be confused, because I'm the one wearing the ring, not you." Jennifer flaunted her wedding ring in my face.

The crowd roared. I wanted to jab Jennifer in the jaw. If what she was telling me was true, Montel had been playing me this whole time. I wanted to kill him. I was speechless.

Vicki asked me if I was all right. I nodded. Jennifer sat there with the look of Victory on her face. All I could do was fight back. I started shouting out dates, personal things that we shared. If Montel played me, he was playing her too, and she was the bigger idiot because she married the fool!

"Well you know what, Jennifer? That was your mistake. You married a dog, who has been lying to me, and is obviously still lying to you. I was with him, so just get over it!"

Vicki tried to take control of the audience who disapproved of my adultery. "So Jennifer, how did you find out about Sasha?"

"She left a message on his pager back in December about how she couldn't do this anymore and that she was going to stop seeing him. I asked him about it, he denied it. So months went by, we argued every day. I didn't know who she was to confront her, so I just went by what he said. He told me how she wanted him to leave me and start a family with her. He told me how he and she were just friends and she wanted it to be more, but he wasn't having it. So a couple of months ago, I found reservations to Hawaii for two. I asked him about it. He told me it was a surprise for him and me. After the trip, his credit card bill came, and there were three tickets to Hawaii charged. So I called to clear things up to explain that only two people went. The representative assured me that three tickets were purchased. I called his travel agent and she told me that Montel had purchased two tickets, one for him, and the other for Sasha Freeman. He later purchased one for me. I realized that Sasha was the same Sasha who taught the Lamaze classes, and just took it from there."

The audience roared. I wanted to cry, but I was too damn angry.

Vicki turned to me. "So you and Montel had plans to go to Hawaii?"

"Yes we did. He never showed at the airport, and I haven't heard from him since."

"I see," Vicki said. "Well audience, I think it's time we meet Montel."

The crowd roared. Montel came out with a blindfold on and the audience booed him. He took his blindfold off and turned to his left, he saw me, then he turned to his right and saw Jennifer. He began to sink deep in his chair.

Vicki said, "So Montel, do you know these women?"

He nodded.

"Jennifer tells us you two were happily married until Sasha came along and broke up your family. Sasha tells us, you and she were happy until Jennifer came along and broke up your relationship. What is your story?"

“I’m married to Jennifer. That says it all, right, Vicki?”

The audience booed him. I tried to keep my composure but I was crazy now. This muthafucka came all the way out here, lying, lying to me for months, and had the audacity to disrespect me. I smacked him. Jennifer, tried to throw a blow at me, but I ducked and smacked Montel again. I stood up ready for war. Security flooded the stage. Holding Jennifer back, like little miss house wife was going to do something.

“We cannot have violence on the show,” Vicki said.

We took a break; god knows I needed one from this mess. I couldn’t believe it. The man I loved for so long was a fake, a phony. He faked all his feelings for me, all this love, all this happiness. Montel had fronted all this time. I thought we were so happy, so meant to be. The entire time we spent together was a lie. Montel was just another sorry-ass excuse for a man, trying to get in where he fit in. Well, I wasn’t going down like this. If my ship was sinking, so was everyone else’s. If I didn’t know anything else, the only winner leaving here was going to be me.

The show started back up. I was calm and quiet. I didn’t even look Jennifer or Montel’s way, the so-called happy couple. What bullshit, Montel didn’t deserve anyone, not even a pet dog. Vicki reiterated the fact that there could be no violence on the show. I agreed. I got all my licks in. I was ready for verbal blows at this point and I would be the only one throwing them. The show began. Vicki decided to hear from the audience. Just then, I knew things would be going my way, because I had my girls in the audience and they knew just what to do.

Vicki walked through the audience, who had their hands raised. One lady, who looked about twenty, stood up and ignorantly said, "If I were you girl, I'd beat her ass for sleeping with your husband, and then I'd kick his ass for sleeping with her."

The audience roared. Vicki started egging people, as if she wanted to keep those comments coming. Another girl, who looked about twelve, stood up and said, "Sister girl, she isn't even worth all that, just kick him to the curb!"

Another middle-aged woman said, "See this is the problem with the institution of marriage these days amongst young people, y'all don't have any respect for each other. What about your child you have together?"

I felt like saying to that damn lady, look around, sister, the institution of marriage isn't just fucked up in young people. Where is your husband? Anyways, a couple of votes for Jennifer's side started to die down, when the brothers spoke.

One man said, "Montel is a dog and deserves no one."

Another man said, "Jennifer was stupid for marrying him."

Another man from the crowd asked if he could meet me after the show because I was fine-ass shit. Some diva-decked-out sister said, "If he was with her, obviously something isn't right in your marriage, take a closer look."

Finally, Lisa stood up and defended her girl. "Vicki, I am going to tell you something right now. I know Sasha, and I know Montel. The bottom line is, the relationship they had was real. He continued to come around after he was married, despite his commitment to Jennifer. Sasha didn't even know the brother was getting married until someone told her. Montel has stayed over

Sash's house; they have gone to L.A. together, other trips and so forth. So if Jennifer even believes one word that lying son of a bitch has to say, that is on her."

The crowd clapped at Lisa's speech. I was starting to feel vindicated.

Vicki directed the questioning back to me. "Is that true, Sasha, you and Montel had a serious relationship?"

"Yes, Vicki, that is true."

"And you thought it was just you and him going to Hawaii?"

"Yep." I turned to Jennifer. "Look girlfriend, I could care less what you do with your life, but don't you ever come to me with this bullshit again. The fact of the matter is that Montel is dogging you, and you are the idiot defending him. It's okay, because lord knows he has snowed me too. But the good thing is, I'm not anymore. You can keep your husband, just keep him the hell away from me!"

The crowd clapped. Jennifer began to respond, but I cut her off. "And another thing, if you are so secure in your marriage and Montel is so faithful, why is there a me at all?"

Jennifer said, "Look, Sasha, I came out here today upset. I needed someone else to blame, I needed something else to be true besides the fact that my husband is not the man I thought he was. I wanted answers, and I got them."

Jennifer turned to Montel. "I hope you brought enough money with you because the locks are being changed as we speak, and I want your lying, cheating, no good pitiful excuse for a husband out of my house. Goodbye!"

The crowd exploded! Montel didn't say anything, he just looked as if Jennifer's words were not true and he could talk his way out of this one. Jennifer's eyes had been familiar eyes. Eyes that I saw in Lisa, when she was finished with Jake. Eyes, that I had seen in Michelle when she threw Jamal out. Eyes I had seen in T when she gave up on Ricky. Eyes that stared back at me, when I looked in the mirror and realized that I had been snowed, and I wasn't going to take it anymore.

After the show, I left quickly. I didn't want to see or hear another word. I told Vicki she could speak to my lawyers, if I see this show on TV in a distasteful manner. I gathered the ladies together and dashed to the airport to find the first available flight to Boston. I couldn't wait to get out of this hell. On the plane ride back, the ladies filled me in on what happened before I came onto the show. Jennifer was bad mouthing me, making it seem like I stole her husband. They were so shocked and tried to get backstage to warn me, but security wouldn't let them through. I held my head high. It was inevitable. I did do wrong on my part by sleeping with Montel when I knew he was married, that one time. But damn, he has been lying from jump. It made me wonder about my judgment of men. I don't think I can pick them. Oh well, what next.

I couldn't reach my house porch fast enough. I was so tired. The plane ride was so exhausting. I couldn't wait to get in my bed and go to sleep. My porch light was out. Great, another thing I would have to fix, besides my personal life. Well, one good thing came out of this. I finally got some closure. I wouldn't waste my time on loving Montel anymore. I thought I would be more upset than this, but I wasn't. I guess I was used to the let down, the disappointment. Whatever, life does go on. I didn't see Raymond's car in the driveway, it was late, where could he be? Anyway, I struggled with the door keyhole because of the darkness. The cool fall breeze crept up on my shoulder. I felt someone watching me. I turned around. No one was there. I opened my door. Then I heard quick steps coming up my stairway. I was frightened, I thought it was Raymond, but to my horror, it was an all too familiar and unwanted face. It was Jason, the lunatic.

"Hi, Sasha, how you doing."

I was startled and afraid, but tried to keep my composure, so he didn't see how scared I was. "What the fuck are you doing here, I have a restraining order on you."

"You did have one on me but that ended months ago."

"Whatever, you are not wanted here, so leave!"

"I'm not trying to cause you harm. I just wanted to…" He paused as tremors took over his hands. "I just wanted to apologize first for my behavior. Secondly, I want to thank you for your help. I know now that it was you who referred me to those psychiatrists. They really helped me. I been trying to call you, but I never have the nerve to say anything."

I thought *the hang-ups, shit I never did change my number, he still has it. But where has he been all this time? Has he been waiting to get me alone, to make his move? What the fuck does he want?* "Look, Jason, I appreciate the apology, and I saw that you needed help. I just was trying to do my part that's all."

"Well, you did, and I am better now."

"That's good to know. Well, I have to be going, so if you don't mind…"

"I know Sasha, you probably have a laundry list of men trying to get at you, so I won't waste your time. I just wanted to know, one thing first."

I knew I would regret this, but I asked the question. "What?"

"Why, was it never me? All these dudes I've seen you with, all these relationships, how come you never gave us a chance?"

"You're not my type."

Jason's hands started to tremble again, his voice changed from calm, to erratic. He started asking questions, and answering himself. "Well, why didn't you give me a chance? Oh that's right, I am not your type."

He continued talking to himself. He was freaking me out. I started to grab for my mace just in case he got out of order. He grabbed my arm as if he knew what I was up to.

"Sasha, all I wanted was a chance, a chance for us."

"Let go of my fucking arm, all right?"

I was trying to sound like I was in control. With his arm, he held my wrist real tight, and with his other hand he pulled out a knife.

I was hysterical. "What the hell are you doing?" I cried.

"I just wanted you to listen, I just wanted you to see that you and me should be together."

"What! By holding a knife to my throat? You are crazy."

"Open your door, Sasha," Jason demanded.

"No!"

"Open, the door and let me in!"

"No!" I cried.

He pressed his pelvis against me as he slammed my back to the door. He tried to snatch the keys to my house out of my hand. I threw them in the yard.

"You're going to pay for that one bitch!" He pointed the knife in my direction as he said that.

I didn't know his next move. Craziness was in his eyes. He ripped open my coat and began to kiss my neck and fondle my breast. His knife was against my throat. There I was, pinned up against my own front door, about to be raped by a fucking psycho. I had to think fast. Before I could get my knee up to kick him where it hurts, he was tossed off of me, and thrown to the ground. I thought it was Raymond. But to my surprise and joy, it was Michael. To my rescue once again.

Jason was hauled off to jail, again. I filed a statement at the police station, again. Turns out, Jason had been in an institution for the mentally ill for the past year, and he escaped. He was diagnosed with Schizophrenia. My luck, Michael knew he had escaped, and knew the first place he would go, my house. Michael didn't say anything to me. He made it seem as if he was only after the bad guy. He showed no emotion, no interest in me at all. In fact, he had some other officer take my statement. I wanted to thank him, but feared I wouldn't get the chance. All these months of getting over hurt had silenced him. He was cold. He reminded me of T, when Ricky left her standing at the alter. He hated me, I knew it.

But I had to let him know that I was thankful he showed up when he did, no matter how he felt about me. As I was leaving he and a couple of other doughnut lovers were sitting around laughing. When I walked by him, he had his back turned toward me. I wanted to hug him; I wanted to kiss him, but feared rejection. I walked out of the station, alone.

CHAPTER TWENTY-FOUR

So months later, and then years later, I still know what is true. It's like making a bowl of rice pudding. You know what ingredients to use to make this fabulous dish. You know how to prepare for it, cook it, cool it and eat it. To your sweet delight it could taste just right, or could need a few things to make it just right. Nonetheless, you can do two things with the rice, eat it, and keep adding ingredients, so it eventually taste right, or you can throw the rice pudding away, and make a new batch.

Lisa chose to keep her rice pudding, she found in Damon. The past was the past. Honestly, she couldn't say she wasn't happier than she ever had been. Although, Damon was the finest thing that ever walked this earth in my opinion, he had faults and weaknesses, things that would make me throw him away and start a new batch. But not, Lisa. To her, he was just right, even if she had to compromise at times. There were times when her insecurities controlled her, or self-esteem issues made her feel vulnerable and so uneasy. Damon and Lisa weren't snowed. What they felt for each other was real, and no one was playing any games. No one was pretending to feel one way, when they really didn't feel that way at all. No one was controlling the other's feelings, and at the same time masking their feelings, so that the other person couldn't really see what was going on. Both Lisa and Damon's eyes and heads were clear and they knew what they had found in each other. That is why they are still together today and in love more than anyone could know.

A knocking came over my door. I wanted to get this speech down pat before the reception; I couldn't let my girl down. The knocking got louder and louder. "Damn it, I am coming hold on, I will be there in a minute."

It was Raymond. He was wearing his tuxedo, and shiny black shoes. I thought it was nice of Lisa to want him in the wedding. After all, he had been like a second brother to her, since we were so close. It was Raymond's responsibility to make sure, the bridesmaids and grooms got to the wedding on time. He and his son, now five, were looking too handsome. I snapped a picture, and tried to put it to my memory. The two most important men in my life, my brother and my nephew. Sometimes, it seemed like the only men. I had my share though. I thought I would never get it together. There are days when I don't think I will ever get this relationship crap right. Here I was thirty-four, going to another wedding, where I was in the party, but nowhere near getting married. I thought I would be by now. I thought I would find the perfect, ideal man. It wasn't until I met Montel, that I realized the ideal man, is what you make him.

Montel, someone, I had not thought about in years. He changed something in me. He made me lose my trust in men, and gain more trust in me. I don't regret anything that happened, I'm grateful, that I got out before it was too late.

It wasn't too late for Michelle. She would be a bridesmaid as well. She was once a bride, but realized the happy ending she expected was a nightmare. A nightmare she created because she couldn't see the truth. Well, Michelle got through a long hard storm and is enjoying the cool spring breeze. She dates here and there, but never gives herself up completely. She lets men know her issues upfront, and if they can't handle it, cool, they can just be friends.

Tamieka has done a lot of that through the years. Just keeping it simple, just being friends. She met this man named Ron when she flew off to Jamaica one year. He lives in D.C. so their relationship is somewhat distant. Their friendship/courtship has lasted for three years now. That is a record for T. She is actually being friends with a man, expecting nothing, desiring all, but contending to none. Their relationship, from my eyes, is built on a long history of respect.

Respect, that's something I thought Montel and I had for one another. Boy was I wrong. I never spoke to him again, after that day on the show. I had my closure, before my opening with him. I gave him chances after chances, concealing what I knew as true, and being open to what I knew was false. I did that to myself. The last I heard of Montel, he and Jennifer were still married, working on their third child, and Montel was the stay home mom taking care of them. I had to wonder what went through Jennifer's head? She was still snowed, maybe one day she would see, like Michelle did, after child and tribulation number three.

The limo was going too fast. I couldn't jot my speech down in my head. I wanted to say so much about Lisa and Damon; I just didn't know where I would start. They had surpassed a lot of obstacles and still remained together. Damon was such a lady's man, how could Lisa fall for him? I guess Damon saw in Lisa what she saw in him, hope.

"Damn it, if this Limo goes over one more bump, I am going to throw my pumps at him," I declared.

"Stop your moaning, Sasha, we're almost there," Lisa said in a calm voice. She was so nervous about her wedding. Her dress was Vera Wang, white, halter-top design. "Sasha, you can't keep complaining like this, it is my day, not Sash's day to bitch and moan."

"Fine," I said, with an attitude.

Lisa grabbed my hand. "I need you today girl, I can't do this alone."

"Need who?" T said in a burst. "If I recall correctly we are all, in this together."

"The wedding, yes, not the honeymoon." Michelle giggled. Michelle seemed so full of life, after she left Jamal. She was more secure in herself, more secure in the good in people, rather than the good they saw in her. T wanted to toast of course. Three drunken bridesmaids and one bride didn't quite look right. T had slowed a lot on her drinking and smoking since her quiet storm. She too, seemed brighter in a sense.

Lisa took a deep breath and decided to say a speech before we got to the church. "Ladies, hear me when I say this. I couldn't have gotten here without you. You were there when I was weak, there when I was dumb and there when I was lost. Now, I have stumbled across something so wonderful, I can't help but be thankful. I found happiness in life, and I owe that to you. Sasha, don't worry about your speech, just let it flow, like that, from the heart."

The Limo pulled up to the church. Not all the guests were inside yet. The groomsman went in first, and the bride and her party sat in the limo, while we waited for everyone to go inside. I searched thoughts after thoughts trying to come up with something that said Damon and Lisa belonged together. Thoughts just didn't flow into words. I was missing something.

As I looked out the tinted window, I saw a familiar face. He was six-feet tall, dark skin with white pearly teeth. He smiled at me, as if he could see me. I smiled back at him as if he could see me. Michael always knew how to make me feel happy again, feel like myself, no bullshit, and no games. He stayed around, just as friends though. Michael was one of the best friends I had. We could shoot pool together, watch movies, eat out, talk shit, and still call each other the next day. It was like we were old friends since we were kids. Michael would never get intimate with me like that ever again. We were bad for each other in that way. I hurt him and he loved me. That is how that relationship would work. So friends it was, and has been ever since that night he saved me from Jason. He showed up at my house and we talked. Somehow we stayed in touch and stayed close friends rather than lovers.

So there he was, this man, who probably would be the only man to love me like this. Probably the only man who could and I let him go. I let him get hurt and caught up in the game. If two people were meant to be together, then they would be. Lisa and Damon made it through the long haul. Suddenly, what I said at Lisa's reception didn't matter so much. Them getting married said it all. Love was winning today. I don't know who would win tomorrow, but love was winning today. And that is all that needed to be said on my part.

As for Michael and me, if we were meant to be, then we would be. Like I said, nothing but love was ruling this day. Fear cometh, worries cometh, doubts cometh, but when two people are really in love, there's no room for being snowed, just room to be in love with one another come rain, snow or high water. When it comes down to it, you just have to know when to keep the good batch and when to throw the bad ones away.

THE END

Available for ordering online at:

www.kindleeyesbooks.com

www.amazon.com

www.bn.com

www.borders.com

www.theblacklibrary.com

www.jamaicawaybooks.com

or by mail:

Name:________________________________

Address:____

# of copies__________

Price $10 per copy plus 2.95(per copy) shipping and handling

Mail To:

Kindle Eyes Books

PO Box 692092

Quincy MA

02669

Wholesalers and Bookstores contact Ingram Book Distributors

Book Club and Bulk orders receive 20% Discount(order via www.kindleeyesbooks.com or submit this order form)

Printed in the United States
67131LVS00003B/346

9 780615 12111